# "WE BELIEVE..."

A Survey

of the

## CATHOLIC
## FAITH

Revised and Cross-Referenced to the
*Catechism of the Catholic Church*

Father Oscar Lukefahr, C.M.

Foreword by Archbishop Justin Rigali

**LIGUORI**
PUBLICATIONS

One Liguori Drive
Liguori, MO 63057-9999
(314) 464-2500

ISBN 0-89243-536-4
Library of Congress Catalog Card Number: 95-76122

Copyright © 1990, Oscar Lukefahr, C.M.
Printed in the United States of America
Revised Edition 1995
95 96 97 98 99   5 4 3 2 1

Scripture quotations are taken from the *New American Bible*, Copyright © 1970, 1986, and 1991 by the Confraternity of Christian Doctrine, 3211 Fourth Street, N.E., Washington, DC 20017-1194, and are used with permission. All rights reserved.

Excerpts from the English translation of the *Catechism of the Catholic Church* for the United States of America, copyright © 1994, United States Catholic Conference, Inc.–Libreria Editrice Vaticana. Used with permission.

Excerpts from the English translation of *Rite of Baptism for Children,* copyright © 1969, International Committee on English in the Liturgy, Inc. (ICEL); excerpts from the English translation of *Rite of Penance,* copyright © 1974 (ICEL); excerpts from the English translation of *Rite of Confirmation,* Second Editon, copyright © 1975 (ICEL); and excerpts from the English translation of *Pastoral Care of the Sick: Rites of Anointing and Viaticum,* copyright © 1982 (ICEL), are used with permission.

Cover photograph copyright © 1995 by The Order of St. Benedict, Inc. Published by The Liturgical Press, Collegeville, Minnesota. Used with permission.

Cover design by Myra Roth

# "WE BELIEVE..."

# OTHER WORKS BY
# OSCAR LUKEFAHR, C.M.

A Catholic Guide to the Bible

The Privilege of Being Catholic

Morning Star…Christ's Mother and Ours

*Workbooks also available*

# DEDICATION

*To my mother, Marie Lukefahr,*
*who first taught me to know and love Jesus,*
*and to all my family.*

# CONTENTS

## PART II: WORSHIP

## PART III: CHRISTIAN LIFE

## PART IV: PRAYER

# Foreword

Today's growing desire for a solid and exact knowledge of the content of our faith is evident in the phenomenal worldwide demand for the recently published *Catechism of the Catholic Church.* The purpose of the *Catechism* is to present "an organic synthesis of the essential and fundamental contents of the Catholic doctrine, as regards both faith and morals, in light of the Second Vatican Council and the whole of the Church's Tradition."[1]

The *Catechism*, while being highly recommended reading for all the faithful, was primarily intended for those responsible for teaching the faith—bishops, priests, and catechists.[2] In the Prologue of the *Catechism*, we find an acknowledgment of its own limitations: "By design, this Catechism does not set out to provide the adaptation of doctrinal presentations and catechetical methods required by the differences of culture, age, spiritual maturity, and social and ecclesial condition among all those to whom it is addressed."[3]

Father Oscar Lukefahr, C.M., in *"We Believe..." A Survey of the Catholic Faith* takes much of the content of the *Catechism* and articulates it in a readily understandable manner. *"We Believe..."* presents Catholic doctrine and its application in a concise and attractive fashion. Father Lukefahr in the current edition has enhanced the usefulness of *"We Believe..."* by providing cross-references to the *Catechism*, the normative and authentic statement of faith for our day.

*"We Believe..."* provides an overview of Catholic belief, which is helpful to the non-Catholic inquirer as well as the cradle Catho-

---

[1]*Catechism of the Catholic Church*, Prologue, #11.
[2]*Catechism of the Catholic Church*, Prologue, #12.
[3]*Catechism of the Catholic Church*, Prologue, #24.

lic who is seeking a deeper and more coherent understanding of Catholicism. Father Lukefahr not only faithfully expresses Catholic teaching on the controversial issues of the day (that is, infallibility, divorce, family planning, purgatory, and so on), but he provides thoughtful reasons and support data, which make understandable the Church's teaching and reveal the flaws of contemporary challenges to Catholic doctrine.

Pope John Paul II in the Apostolic Constitution *Fidei Depositum*, which begins the *Catechism*, prays: "May the light of the true faith free humanity from the ignorance and slavery of sin in order to lead it to the only freedom worthy of the name (cf. John 8:32): that of life in Jesus Christ under the guidance of the Holy Spirit, here below and in the Kingdom of heaven, in the fullness of the blessed vision of God face to face (cf. 1 Corinthians 13:12; 2 Corinthians 5:6-8)![4] It is with that same hope that I recommend this book to teachers and catechists, to Catholics wishing to deepen their knowledge of faith, and to all earnest seekers of truth. May it bring the light of truth to many minds and its joy to many hearts.

MOST REVEREND JUSTIN RIGALI
ARCHBISHOP OF ST. LOUIS
FEBRUARY 22, 1995

---

[4]*Catechism of the Catholic Church*, Apostolic Constitution *Fidei Depositum*, United States Catholic Conference, p. 6.

# Introduction

The greatest adventure we face as human beings is to explore the meaning of life. Questions like "Where does the universe come from?" and "Is there a God?" and "What happens to us when we die?" challenge us to think, love, and live. It is the conviction of Catholic Christians that the answers to these questions are found in Jesus Christ. This book has been written to explain how Catholics follow Jesus in thinking about the meaning of existence, in loving God and neighbor, and in experiencing life as a gift from God.

I have tried to be faithful to authentic Catholic teaching as it is rooted in Scripture and sacred Tradition. Bible passages are quoted frequently. The *Catechism of the Catholic Church* and the documents of the Second Vatican Council provide the foundation for the development of each chapter. This second edition follows the four main divisions of the *Catechism*: **belief**, **worship**, **Christian life**, and **prayer**. Chapter subheadings are cross-referenced to the *Catechism* so that readers who want to study a particular topic in the *Catechism* may easily do so. (For example, "C 1-26" refers to Sections 1-26 of the *Catechism*.)

*"We Believe..."* is intended for those interested in joining the Catholic Church and for Catholics who wish to increase their understanding of their faith. It can be useful for adult-religious education classes, RCIA programs, Catholic high school and CCD religion classes, college classes, discussion groups, and private study. I have tried to make it long enough to provide a survey of the important aspects of Catholicism but brief enough to allow busy people to read it in a reasonable amount of time.

Religious education is a matter not only of the head but also of the heart. I pray that this book may help people *know about* Jesus Christ and the teachings of the Catholic Church. I pray that it may help people *know and love* Jesus Christ as Savior, Friend, Lord and God, to commit their lives to him, and to be active members of his Church.

"And this is my prayer: that your love may increase ever more and more in knowledge and every kind of perception, to discern what is of value, so that you may be pure and blameless for the day of Christ" (Philippians 1:9-10).

FATHER OSCAR LUKEFAHR, C.M.

P.S. This book has been developed out of my experiences of more than twenty-five years as a priest and teacher of religious education. I am indebted to the Daughters of Charity, who taught me in grade school; to the seminary professors and authors, especially those listed in the Bibliography, who have helped form my understanding of Jesus Christ and his Church.

I want to express gratitude to Cecelia Portlock, Father Robert Pagliari, C.SS.R., Kass Dotterweich, and to the editorial staff at Liguori Publications for assistance and support. I am grateful to Jim and Toni Walters, who first encouraged me to write for Liguori; to Paul and Carol Berens, who proofread the manuscript; to my Vincentian confreres and to priests of the diocese of Springfield-Cape Girardeau for their advice and suggestions; to the parishioners at St. Denis Church in Benton, Missouri, especially those who attended the pilot project class for this book; to the members of Most Precious Blood Church in Denver, Colorado, and St. Vincent de Paul Church in Cape Girardeau, Missouri; to the Cape Girardeau discussion group; to my family; to Father Robert Brockland, C.M., and Father William McEvoy, who made many helpful suggestions for the second edition, and to Joan Ruhl, who proofread the second edition. May God bless you all!

# PART I
# BELIEF

# CHAPTER ONE
# Our World and Our God

How did our universe come to be? When did life begin? Is there a God? Could everything have come from nothing? Is there a meaning or purpose to life? How can we find true happiness? What happens to us when we die? These are the most basic questions that face us as human beings, and people have wondered about them for ages.

Ancient cave drawings and burial sites indicate that early humans believed in deities and in life after death. Today polls show that most human beings believe in God and in eternal life. But some people believe there is no God, no purpose to life, and no life after death. We believe in God or in "nothing" as the Ultimate Reality. In spite of scientific advances, we still must "believe."

### The Need to Believe (C 27–30)

Why must we believe? Some knowledge can be obtained through our senses or by scientific investigation. We don't have to believe that apples are red. We can see that. We don't have to believe that water is made up of two parts of hydrogen and one part of oxygen. We can establish that by scientific investigation.

But the knowledge essential in life and the answers to questions about Ultimate Reality can be acquired only by faith. For example, psychologists say that to be happy we must love and be loved. We cannot prove scientifically that others love us. We must either believe it or go through life without love. We'll never be able to put love under a microscope, but we can see that believing in love is worthwhile because love enriches our lives. The emptiness of a loveless life and the joy of a love-filled life demonstrate that love is real.

So it is with faith in God. We can't put God under a microscope. (If we could, God would be just a part of our limited material world.) We can't have scientific proof that God exists and is the origin of the universe. On the other hand, we can't have scientific proof that nothing is behind the universe because we can't put nothing under a microscope either! Ultimately, we must believe in God or in nothing.

### Reasons for Belief in God (C 31–35)

If we choose to believe in God rather than nothing, what are the reasons? Many have been given, and we will focus on three of them.

The first is that the universe must come either from a God who put it into being or it must come from nothing. There are no other alternatives. To most human beings it is more reasonable to believe that the universe comes from Someone than to believe that it comes from nothing. If there is no Creator, why does anything exist? A philosophical argument puts it this way: "Why is there something rather than nothing? The universe as we know it exists without a sufficient reason for existing. Its only sufficient reason must be in Another, a Being beyond the world, supernatural, namely God."

The second reason is built around the laws of chance. Chance means that something occurs without intention or cause. For example, if I take ten coins dated 1971 to 1980 and try to draw 1971 without searching for it, I depend on chance. If so, the "odds" are ten to one. If I try to draw 1971 and 1972 in order, the odds jump to one hundred to one (assuming that I return each coin after it is drawn). The odds against pulling out 1971 to 1980 in order are ten billion to one! What would the odds be that the whole universe could have been formed by accident, by chance? Truly incredible! If there were no God, everything would have to be an accident. Few people would bet that anyone could drop a bomb on a junkyard and produce a *Boeing 747* or throw a stick of dynamite into a print shop and create Webster's dictionary! But the odds for this happening are better than the odds of producing an entire universe by accident. That is why some thinkers feel that it is reasonable to believe in God from the laws of chance alone.

The third reason has to do with us. Nothing in this world can bring us complete happiness. Life doesn't make sense unless we are moving toward a God who will give us what we long for. As Saint Augustine said: "You have made us for yourself, O Lord, and our hearts are restless until they rest in you." We have a hunger deep inside that this world cannot fill because it is meant to be filled by God. Further, belief in God makes sense because it brings out the best in us. When we see how belief in God is the foundation of the beautiful lives of people like Mother Teresa of Calcutta, we realize that it makes us better than we would be otherwise. We can be fully human only when we believe in God.

So just as we make a choice to accept love, so we make a decision to accept belief in God. As a life without love is shriveled and weak, so a life without belief in God is hollow and empty. As love enriches life, so faith in God enriches life. It is reasonable to believe in God. And when we say, "We believe in God," we are making a positive statement about life and about ourselves. Life has meaning because it comes from God. We are not accidents but God's children. Faith in God is a positive stance which can only enrich our lives as human beings.

## The *Catechism of the Catholic Church* (C 1–26)

What the Catholic Church believes about God and the meaning of life is found in the *Catechism of the Catholic Church*. Published in English on June 22, 1994, the *Catechism* is important and valuable for every believer because it takes the wisdom distilled from twenty centuries of humanity's quest for God and places it in our hands. It gathers Church teaching from many sources into one volume.

In a certain sense, it is a catechism of the Second Vatican Council, a gathering of bishops in Rome from 1962 to 1965. It arranges the teachings of the Council in logical order for study and reflection. It integrates them with the great sources of belief such as the Bible, the liturgy, instructions of previous Church councils and popes, and the works of prominent theologians.

The *Catechism* is not a revision of the basic teachings of the Church. The Catholic Church believes that the fundamental truths found in the Bible and sacred Tradition of the Church cannot be changed. But the Church can grow in its understanding of these truths and can improve the clarity with which it expresses them. The Church must constantly apply its teachings to ever changing situations. The *Catechism* expresses ancient truths in modern language, and applies basic principles to today's issues, problems like organ transplants, artificial insemination, and the limits of medical research.

As the Prologue to the *Catechism* states, it is intended primarily for bishops, priests, catechists, and publishers. It is quite lengthy (688 pages of text) and is not meant to replace local catechisms. It may be used as a reference work, like an encyclopedia, and can be read with profit by anyone willing to devote time and effort. Readers of *"We Believe..."* are encouraged to use the *Catechism* to study topics of special interest, especially the moral issues discussed in Part III.

## Doubts and Difficulties (C 2123–28)

The reasons for belief in God are convincing, and the *Catechism of the Catholic Church* is an eloquent testimony to the reasonableness of faith. But many believers are troubled by doubt or by the skepticism of nonbelievers. Doubt can arise when we reflect on the evil in the world. The horrors of modern warfare, the sufferings of victims of cancer and other illnesses, the catastrophe of an earthquake can make us wonder why, if there is a good God, such things can happen. Skeptics can mock believers with the notion that a "truly enlightened intellectual" couldn't believe in such a "medieval" notion as God.

Evil and suffering do raise difficult questions about the existence of God. In our time these questions are perhaps more evident than ever because of modern communications; war, sickness, and natural disasters are brought into our living rooms via television. On the other hand, our ability to answer these questions is enhanced by modern Scripture scholarship and by a better understanding of human freedom and the laws of nature. In later chapters we will explore these issues. Here we simply acknowledge that evil and suffering are a part of human life. They raise the most difficult objections to belief that we encounter. In fact, if there were no evil, no suffering, there would perhaps be no unbelief! But we must recall also that great believers have faced up to the worst possible evils and have experienced the presence and strength of God. Maximilian Kolbe in a Nazi concentration camp during World War II suffered torture, degradation, and death; through it all he believed in a good God, and he brought that belief to others who were suffering with him.

Suffering may raise difficult questions, but it need not destroy belief in God. Kolbe and all the martyrs testify that God becomes more present as suffering intensifies. And if believers have to answer the question, "If God exists, why is there evil in the universe?" then nonbelievers must answer a far more difficult question, "If there is no God, why is there good in the universe?"

As to the objection that truly intelligent people couldn't believe, the fact is that many intellectuals and scientists do believe in God. Some of the most brilliant individuals of modern times, like author C.S. Lewis and philosopher Mortimer Adler, have professed belief in God and have written books explaining their belief. There is no statement less enlightened than the one which says that intelligent people do not believe in God!

### Belief in God for the Twentieth Century (C 36–49, 142–65)

What is more, the arguments for believing in the existence of God have, if anything, been strengthened by the discoveries of recent years. Prior to the twentieth century most people thought that the universe was limited to the few thousand stars visible in the nighttime sky. Even astronomers had only vague ideas about the nature of our Milky Way galaxy and were uncertain if other galaxies might exist. That such a small and relatively uncomplicated universe could come about by accident might seem at least remotely possible.

But what was thought to be the universe proved to be only a tiny speck of it. Using tools like radio telescopes, scientists have discovered that the universe is incredibly vast. Astronomers use light-years as a measure of the universe. A light-second is the distance light travels in one second: 186,282 miles. A light-year is the distance light travels in one year: about six trillion miles! We can gain some insight into the distances involved when we consider that our moon is less than two light-seconds away, 240,000 miles, and that the universe is perhaps forty billion light-years across! The star closest to our own sun, Alpha Centauri, is "only" 4.3 light-years away. Yet if astronauts traveled in today's fastest spaceship to Alpha Centauri, it would take one hundred thousand years to arrive! Once there, they would have taken only the first step in our galaxy, which contains more than two hundred billion stars! They would still have the rest of the galaxies in our universe to explore—one hundred billion or so of them! They would encounter brilliant quasars and black holes with gravitational fields so strong that light is pulled into them and space and time are distorted. They would discover galaxies organized into huge structures awesome in their order, gigantic building blocks for our amazing universe.

If our age has uncovered the vastness of the universe, it has also discovered the almost infinite "smallness" of the atom. Scientists have found that everything in the universe is built of incredibly small particles which are as highly organized as the universe. Using electron microscopes, they have found, for example, that the dot of an "i" on this page contains perhaps a million ink molecules. These, in turn, are formed of atoms, each made up of a nucleus surrounded by electrons which whirl around it. The nucleus is made up of protons and neutrons, combinations of yet smaller particles called quarks. Electrons are only one class of subatomic particles called leptons. There is a galaxy in the dot of an "i"!

Every breath we take contains trillions of atoms. We live on a planet surrounded by trillions of stars. We could spend an eternity trying to grasp the smallness of the atomic building blocks of the universe or the vastness of the whole picture. And we would still be left in awe.

If there were no God, all of this would have to come from nothing! All of its organization must be an accident! If we sometimes find it hard to believe in God, then we should try to believe in nothing. Believers in God are sometimes mocked with the notion that they are putting faith in a fairy tale. On the contrary, there is no fairy tale more incredible than that the universe—infinite in its smallness and in its vastness, astonishing in its structure and organization—could come from nothing! The more we know of the magnificence of the universe, the more we are drawn to believe that it must have a Master Architect to design it and a Creator to build it.

As we take a good look at ourselves, small creatures on a small planet in a small solar system in a small galaxy in our vast universe, we discover that we have within us a desire to come to know the One who made us. Doctors and psychologists have learned that our bodies react in a positive or negative way to certain emotions. Fear, self-pity, and despair release chemicals into our systems that can poison us. Faith, hope, love, and peace can make us healthier.

Two people are standing at the grave of a loved one. The first says, "There is no God. I will never see my friend again. Soon I will die and that will be the end of everything." The second says,

"God has brought my friend to eternal life in heaven. When I die, we will be together again. God loves us, and death brings us to eternal life." The first individual is experiencing feelings likely to cause the release of chemicals harmful to the human body; the second is experiencing feelings that promote health. It is almost as if even our bodies are telling us that we are made for belief in God!

### From Now to Yesterday (C 176–84)

So it is reasonable to believe in God, now more than ever! And while our faith is suitable for today, it is not new. We who believe have a family history. Our tradition stretches across the centuries to a man called Abraham, to a people called the Israelites. Their efforts to come to know and to believe in God are recorded in the "family album" we call the Bible. It is to the Bible we now turn in order to explore our roots, to gain a better understanding of our beliefs, and so to strengthen our faith.

### *Questions for Discussion or Reflection*

When have you felt closest to God? When have you experienced the most serious doubts about God's existence? Which of the reasons for belief in God seem most convincing to you? Are there other reasons for belief that are important to you?

### *Activities*

Read Psalm 8 and Psalm 104. Spend a few minutes reflecting on these psalms; then read them again as prayers of praise to God. Close your eyes and think about the universe as astronomers now describe it to us. Picture yourself from some vantage point in space: You are a tiny human being on a tiny planet in the vastness of the universe. Thank and praise God for creation. Ask God to help you realize that God's power includes the ability to pay attention to you and to love you!

# CHAPTER TWO
# Our Religious Tradition

When we reflect on the magnificence of the universe, we can only wonder at how great its Maker must be. As we are dazzled by the marvel of created things, we realize the wisest of us can have only the faintest notion of our Creator. So it is not surprising that human beings have had many diverse opinions about God and have developed many different religious traditions.

Some of these have placed limits on God and have stated that God has weaknesses and cannot satisfy our hopes for perfect happiness. But the Creator of our universe is infinite. Nothing about God is "too good to be true."

## The Judeo-Christian Religious Tradition (C 50–73)

One religious tradition has placed no limits on the greatness of God or on God's ability to fulfill our dreams, the Judeo-Christian tradition.

It begins with Abram, a native of Ur, an ancient city north of the Persian Gulf. In about 1900 B.C., Abram's family migrated to Haran, a city near the present-day Turkish-Syrian border. (All dates in this chapter are B.C. unless otherwise noted.) In Haran, Abram received a call from God to move to Canaan, present-day Palestine. God made a "covenant" (an agreement) with Abram, changing his name to Abraham and promising that he and his wife, Sarah, would have a son, the first in a long line of descendants. They did have a son, Isaac, who in turn became the father of Jacob. Jacob had twelve sons and with them moved to Egypt about 1750, where their descendants, the Hebrews, became slaves.

About 1250 a Hebrew named Moses heard God commanding him to lead his people from slavery in Egypt to freedom in the land of Canaan, the Promised Land. After escaping, the Hebrews (who became known as Israelites and later as Jews) wandered about in the desert for forty years. Moses died on the border of the Promised Land, and his lieutenant, Joshua, led the people into Canaan. There followed a period of conquest, with the twelve tribes (divisions of the Hebrew people named after the sons of Jacob) settling in various parts of Canaan. They fought with the inhabitants (Philistines and others) through a long "frontier period" called the time of the Judges.

About 1020 Saul, a member of the tribe of Benjamin, began to bring the tribes together and was named king. He eventually went insane and was killed in a battle with the Philistines. Into the breach stepped a young military leader, David. Beginning about 1000, David united the tribes, set up Jerusalem as the center of his government, defeated the enemies of the Israelites, and made Israel a force to be reckoned with in the Middle East. His son, Solomon, succeeded him as king and built a magnificent temple in Jerusalem. But in his later years Solomon became involved in the worship of false gods and alienated the people with heavy taxes and forced labor. Solomon's son, Rehoboam, continued these policies, and in 922 (some scholars say 927) a civil war split the people into two kingdoms—Israel in the north with its capital in Samaria, and Judah in the south with its capital in Jerusalem.

Both kingdoms were plagued by poor leadership and by the people's unfaithfulness to God. In 721 the northern kingdom was attacked by Assyria; its leading citizens were slaughtered or dragged into exile. Other captives from foreign lands were brought into Israel by the Assyrians; they intermarried with the few Israelites who had been left behind, forming the people known as the Samaritans. In 587 the southern kingdom was conquered by the Babylonians. Jerusalem was sacked, its walls destroyed, and its temple demolished. The survivors were taken into exile in Babylon.

A few decades later Cyrus, the king of Persia, conquered Babylon. He allowed the Israelites to return to their homeland in 539. Those who returned to Judah found their land devastated, their homes destroyed, and Jerusalem a heap of ruins. Harassed on every side by enemies, they managed to build a temple about 515 and to rebuild the city walls, completing the task in 445. Their hopes of regaining the glory of King David, however, were doomed to disappointment. Alexander the Great conquered Palestine in 332. After Alexander's death, Egypt and Syria vied for control of the Jewish nation, and about 200 the Syrians launched a terrible persecution of the Jews. In 167 a family of warriors, the Maccabees, led a revolt against the Syrians and succeeded in gaining independence in 142. This lasted until 63 when the Romans, under Pompey, conquered Jerusalem and made Palestine a vassal state. In 39 Herod the Great was set up by the Romans as king. A man who committed many horrible atrocities, he was also a tireless builder, constructing fortresses, palaces, and a magnificent temple which outshone that of Solomon. It was under his rule that Jesus Christ was born.

Not a very impressive history! Except for a brief period under King David, the Israelite nation had little political or military influence. But somehow they kept their belief in the God of Abraham. Somehow they kept alive a hope that God would intervene in history by sending a Savior. When God did send that Savior, there were Israelites ready to welcome him.

## The Bible—Origin, Nature, and Interpretation (C 101–19)

Throughout the history of the Israelite people, there were those who were inspired to record their experience of God. History and stories, poetry and preaching, laws and legends, proverbs and prophecy, were passed on from generation to generation. These inspired writings were recognized by spiritual leaders as revelations from God and cherished as God's own Word.

They have come down to us as the books of the Bible. Catholics recognize forty-six books written before Christ as the Old Testament and twenty-seven books written about Christ as the New Testament. The Church believes that these seventy-three books are divinely inspired, that they have God as their Author. This does not mean that God dictated the books, but that God guided the human authors to write in such a way that the books teach religious truth. The human authors played an important part, and we can understand the message of the inspired books only when we have some awareness of who wrote them, when and why they were written, and what the authors intended to convey.

This approach to the Bible is called the "contextual" approach. It means that we must have the context of any given passage if we are to understand it. Another approach to the Bible is the "fundamentalist approach," which states that the words of the Bible must be taken only at face value. If the words say that Jonah was swallowed by a fish and lived in its belly for three days, then such an event occurred. The contextual approach would lead us to study when, where, why, and by whom the book was written and so arrive at the conclusion that Jonah is a parable designed to teach that God loves all nations.

Some people are frightened by the contextual approach and feel that it leads us to treat the whole Bible as a fable. This is not the case. There is history in the Bible, as well as parables, laws, poetry, songs, and many other forms of writing, each of which can teach religious truth in its own way.

We shouldn't be surprised at this because we use the contextual approach every day. For example, any newspaper has the front-page news, editorials, sports, comics, classifieds, and advertisements, and we understand each differently. On the front page we might read the words, "An armed guard gunned down a robber as he tried to steal the company payroll." On the sports page we might read, "The Cincinnati catcher gunned down the St. Louis left fielder as he tried to steal second base." The same words are used, but they have a very different meaning! We don't have any difficulty understanding them (at least if we know something about baseball) because we are aware of the context of each sentence. On the other hand, if we took the second sentence in a fundamentalist fashion, we might be misled to suppose that baseball is a very violent sport!

Learning to read the Bible intelligently is something like reading the newspaper. But because the Bible was written so long ago, in a different culture, we must become acquainted with the "context" of its books. Most Catholic Bibles have introductions that present the information needed, and there are many books (such as *A Catholic Guide to the Bible*, Liguori Publications; see Bibliography) available to make Bible reading easy, enjoyable, and beneficial.

### Reading the Bible (C 129–41)

Another important thing to remember in reading the Bible is that its various books are not organized according to subject matter or chronology. Therefore, it's not best to start on page one and try to read straight through. Many people who do this find themselves bogged down in difficult passages and become discouraged. Readers should first become familiar with the "whole picture," then they can read the Bible with understanding.

Someone who is investigating the Judeo-Christian tradition for the first time and is handed a Bible might be compared to a refugee from a war-torn country who is being adopted into a family. Such a person might be told, "We want you to feel at home, so we are giving you copies of all the documents that relate to our family. Look through them and you'll discover what we are like." The documents might include genealogies, blueprints for the family home, stories told by grandparents, letters written by family members to one another, songs used at family gatherings, and so on. The individual might browse through these documents and find some to be very helpful and others of limited usefulness. Family letters might be essential in giving insight about the love and care of family members for one another. Blueprints, on the other hand, might not be all that interesting, unless the individual being adopted happens to be an architect!

Some parts of the Bible are very important to any believer. The psalms are frequently used in private prayer and public worship. Some parts of the Book of Numbers, with long lists of names and places, might be of interest only to specialists. Once we become familiar with the general structure of the Bible and do some "sampling," we can find those passages which will be most helpful.

## A Global View of the Old Testament (C 121–23)

Geographers today bemoan the fact that many people have little knowledge of our world. Yet knowledge of the earth and of the interrelationship of its parts is crucial to our survival: the burning of the rain forests in Brazil could bring about the melting of polar icecaps and the flooding of New York. We should gain at least a general awareness of the globe, then become more acquainted with our own country.

Similarly, many Christians have little knowledge of the "geography" of the Bible, which is as essential to our spiritual survival as knowledge of the globe is to our physical survival. We need some understanding of the Bible as a whole—a global view. This global view can come through an awareness of the main categories of books in the Bible, of their content, and of when they were written. Such a "view" is presented in the following pages. The categories follow those given in *The New American Bible*. The books of the Bible are listed in the order in which they are found in the Scriptures.

## The Pentateuch

The Pentateuch (from the Greek words for "five" and "books") is the collection of the first five books of the Bible. It includes Genesis, Exodus, Leviticus, Numbers, and Deuteronomy. The Pentateuch is meant to answer the basic questions in life and to explain the origins of the Jewish people. Like many other parts of the Bible, the Pentateuch was not written at one time by one author. Rather, it includes traditions, stories, and historical data passed on by word of mouth from generation to generation, put into written collections from about 1000 to 550, and then edited into its present form between 500 and 400.

*Genesis* reflects the Jewish belief that God created the world and that the world is good. Evil is a result of human sinfulness. When people sin, God calls them back through covenants, inviting them to obedient and loving service. Genesis introduces Abraham, the "Father" of all who believe in the true God. *Exodus* recounts the story of the birth of the Jewish nation as the Hebrews are called out of slavery under the leadership of Moses. *Leviticus* emphasizes the holy nature of God's people. *Numbers* describes the organization of the Jewish nation. *Deuteronomy*, largely in the form of a sermon attributed to Moses, shows the spirit of love and obedience which should characterize the people of the covenant.

## The Historical Books

These books cover the period from the entry of the Israelites into the Promised Land in about 1210 to the end of the Maccabean wars in about 142. They are not to be equated with modern history, for ancient historians did not have printing, videorecorders, and telephones. They did not achieve the accuracy we expect from modern historians and often were not concerned about it. Their primary purpose was to teach the story of the encounter of God and humankind, and their works are called "salvation history" to distinguish them from modern history. Nevertheless, the Bible contains much accurate historical data, and many of the names, places, and events have been verified from other sources.

The *Book of Joshua* continues the story of the Israelite people after the death of Moses. Led into the Promised Land by Joshua, the Israelites warred against the inhabitants and established footholds throughout Palestine. *Judges* describes the time after Joshua's death, a two-hundred-yearlong "frontier" period of war and settlement under leaders called "judges." *Ruth* is a beautiful story about love and loyalty in the life of one of King David's ancestors who lived in that frontier period.

The *First* and *Second Books of Samuel* tell about the last judges, Eli and Samuel, and relate how the Israelites were united in 1020 under Saul, their first king. They then describe the troubled relationship of Saul and David, and the long reign of King David. *First* and *Second Kings* take up the story of David's old age, describe how he was succeeded by Solomon, and explain the long decline of the Jewish people that began after David's death. Significant events of this period were the split of Israel into north and south—the fall of the north to Assyria and that of the south to Babylonia. The *First* and *Second Book of Chronicles* are mostly a theologically oriented repetition of material in the Books of Kings.

The Books of *Ezra* and *Nehemiah* cover the return of the Israelites from exile in Babylon and the rebuilding of the Jerusalem temple and walls. *Tobit*, *Judith*, and *Esther* are the sort of literature we might call "historical novels." They are stories set during the exile and restoration that teach trust, courage, care for others, and the importance of remaining faithful to God.

The *First Book of Maccabees* contains the account of Israel's heroic resistance to the persecution by Antiochus IV, a Syrian king who attempted to abolish Jewish religious practices between 171 and 164, and of the struggle for independence waged by the Jews down to 142. The *Second Book of Maccabees* relates in more detail events already narrated in First Maccabees.

### The Wisdom Books

These books are an inspired search into the meaning of life. Using poetry and proverbs, sayings and songs, they face the problems of our origin and destiny, human suffering, good and evil, right and wrong. They deal with homely everyday situations and with the most critical issues of life and death.

The *Book of Job* is a great poem written around 500. It attacks the theory that all suffering is sent by God as punishment for sin and concludes that we cannot give easy answers to the riddle of suffering. Suffering does not separate us from God, and God's presence can help us accept and overcome it.

The *Book of Psalms* is a collection of one hundred fifty prayers in the form of Hebrew poetry. Most were written in the years between King David and the restoration after the Babylonian exile. They address every human emotion and situation, and vary greatly in style, length, and approach. As Hebrew poetry, they depend on the balance of thoughts rather than on rhyme. A good way to use the psalms is to read through them, keeping a list of those that are meaningful for private prayer and reflection.

The *Book of Proverbs* is a collection of wise sayings. The oldest ones date to before the time of Solomon (970) and the newest to about 400. They cover every subject imaginable, from down-to-earth worldly wisdom to lofty theological reflection. *Ecclesiastes* is a book that points out the limitations of human life and the difficulty of knowing its meaning. The author, unaware of the reality of eternal life, advised his readers to live a moral, balanced life, without expecting too much happiness. Written about 300, it demonstrates our need for the wisdom only Christ can give. The *Song of Songs* is a dramatic poem praising the beauty of human love. Created about 300, it is seen by many commentators as symbolic of the love God has for people. *Wisdom* may be the last book of the Old Testament to have been written. Composed around 75, it presents a philosophical reflection on the meaning of Hebrew history and expresses belief in eternal life. *Sirach* (called in some Bibles *Ecclesiasticus*), written around 180, is a book similar to Proverbs. It organizes sayings according to subject matter on topics from table etiquette to religious worship.

### The Prophets

Many people think of prophets as those who foretell the future. Prophets in the Bible, however, are those who "speak for God," and the prophets were primarily concerned with their own contemporary situations.

The official leaders of the northern and southern kingdoms often failed to give the people proper guidance; as a result, both leaders and common folk turned away from God. The prophets condemned the leaders and warned the people of terrible judgment if they did not return to God. When both kingdoms were destroyed, the prophets encouraged the exiles to turn back to God and hope for a better future, a future which promised a "Messiah," a savior from God.

The *Book of Isaiah* was composed by several authors. The first thirty-nine chapters come from the prophet Isaiah (740-687); mindful of God's holiness, he tried to bring Judah back to the Lord. Chapters 40 to 55 were written by an unknown poet during the Babylonian captivity (586-539) and are noted for the Suffering Servant passages foretelling a Messiah who would suffer for God's people. Chapters 56 to 66 contain poems by unknown prophets who wrote in the spirit of Isaiah. *Jeremiah* (626-585) presents the sermons of a great man who prophesied in Judah during its collapse. It gives much autobiographical data remarkable for its honesty and depth of feeling. *Lamentations* is a collection of poems on the misery caused by the destruction of Jerusalem and the exile (587). *Baruch* is a meditation on the exile and a prayer for forgiveness and restoration; it was written long after the exile, as late as 200. *Ezekiel* (597-550) used dramatic visions, symbolic actions, and picturesque language to encourage the people to be faithful to God during the Babylonian exile. *Daniel* takes its name from its hero rather than its author, who is unknown. It was written around 165 as an "apocalypse," a common literary form from 200 B.C. to A.D. 200, characterized by figurative language, visions, symbols, and stories designed to teach that God cares for the faithful, even in persecution. *Hosea* (750) comes from a prophet in the northern kingdom; his marriage to an unfaithful wife and his willingness to take her back represent God's relationship to the unfaithful Israelites. *Joel* is an apocalyptic work composed about 400, using a terrible plague of locusts as a symbol of impending judgment. *Amos* (750) gives the life, times, and prophecies of a shepherd from Judah who prophesied in Israel during a time of prosperity. He warns that Israel will be punished for its injustice toward the poor and oppressed. *Obadiah* (475) is a short, harsh condemnation of the people of Edom who harassed the Jews after they returned from exile in Babylon. *Jonah* (450) is a parable, not a prophecy. It is meant to show God's love and mercy toward all people, even pagans. The author of *Micah* (725-697) was a prophet who condemned the corrupt leaders of Samaria and Jerusalem and promised that a ruler would be born in Bethlehem who would bring restoration and peace. *Nahum* (612) is a song of joy at the destruction of Nineveh, the capital of Assyria, the savage nation which had destroyed Israel and ravaged Judah. *Habakkuk* (600) foretold that Babylon would conquer Judah but that God would use the occasion to purify the Israelites and restore the covenant. *Zephaniah* (620-600) prophesied judgment against Jerusalem at a time when many Jews had gone over to pagan worship. The book looks forward to better days when God's people would respond to divine love and mercy. *Haggai* (520) encouraged the Jews who had returned from exile in Babylon to rebuild the temple and to trust in God. *Zechariah* (520), through a series of visions, also urged the returning exiles to rebuild the temple. The second part of the book was written by unknown authors and foretells the coming of the Prince of Peace. *Malachi* (450) is the last book in the Old Testament (though not the last to be written). It shows the need for constant reform and looks forward to the coming of the Messiah.

## From Good to Bad to Hope for Better (C 362–406)

The Old Testament begins in Genesis with a clear statement that all God creates is good (Genesis 1:31). It acknowledges that human beings experience evil. Suffering, disease, poverty, failure, crime, war, and death are as much a part of the Old Testament as of today's news. All such evils, according to the Old Testament, are the result of human sin.

Sin is the refusal of human beings to obey God. The dramatic story of Adam and Eve, which is not just about the first man and woman but about us all (Genesis 2:4-3:24), shows how human sinfulness introduced evil into the world.

Genesis says that God created people as free, intelligent beings and invited them to accept God's friendship. God told the first humans not to eat from the tree of knowledge of good and bad. This symbolically expressed their obligation to accept God's laws. But they disobeyed God. They sinned, separating themselves from God and losing many of the gifts God had granted them.

Because Adam and Eve were parents of humanity, their sin weakened the human nature they passed on to their descendants. They "transmitted" the condition known as original sin. Original sin did not make humanity or the world wholly evil, but it damaged us in many ways. Original sin deprived us of the union with God and the holiness granted to the first human beings. It made us subject to suffering and death, unable to attain eternal life. It weighed us down with the tendency to do evil instead of good. It damaged our ability to live in harmony with one another and with nature.

Unfortunately, people repeated the disobedience of Adam and Eve in a futile pattern of weakness and evil. What could have been paradise became a world hopelessly immersed in sin.

It was a situation we could not remedy. Finite human beings could not atone for disobedience to an infinite Being. We could not reach up to God and restore the relationship between ourselves and God any more than we could touch the stars. The love relationship between God and us could be restored only if God would reach down to us.

The Old Testament promised that God would indeed reach down by sending a Messiah, a Savior. It closed with a pledge that God would send a prophet to prepare people for the coming of that Savior (Malachi 3:23-24).

## The Old Testament and the Human Condition (C 407–21)

The Old Testament is as honest a presentation of the human condition as can be found. Life as we experience it is neither all good nor all bad. And in the worst of times, most people are able to find hope for the future—usually with an awareness that doom is possible if we repeat the mistakes of the past.

The people of the Old Testament are just like us. We see the foolish mistakes and sins of their political and religious leaders repeated in the follies of some of the political and religious leaders of our day. Samson and Delilah, Saul, David and Bathsheba, Solomon—all have parallels in our time, and in every age. We see the faith of Abraham and the courage of Moses in people of today who trust and serve the Lord. We see ourselves in page after page of the Old Testament as we seek out the good in life and turn away from the bad. We find reason to hope in the future because the hopes of the Jewish people for a Messiah have been fulfilled—in Jesus Christ.

### *Questions for Discussion or Reflection*

Have you read the Old Testament? If not, what have been the obstacles? When you read the Bible or hear it, do you consciously think of it as God speaking to you? The Old Testament is read often at the Mass. Do you know where passages from the Old Testament are used at Mass?

A retreat master asked: "When you stand before God at your judgment, what will be your response when God asks you, 'How did you like my Book?'" What will be *your* response if God asks you this question?

Open your Bible and page through the Old Testament. Note the main categories of books and their length. Read a few introductions. Read some passages you are familiar with. Choose a book; read it from start to finish. Ask God to give you a great love for the Bible and a real sense of belonging to the Judeo-Christian family, with its rich heritage, history, and traditions.

Reflect: you have just been adopted into God's family. Jesus stands before you, gives you the Bible, and says, "I want you to feel at home, so I am giving you all the documents that relate to our family. Look through them and you'll learn what we are like." Take the Bible from his hands, then sit quietly and observe your feelings. Talk to Jesus about them.

## *Try to become familiar with these important dates:*

**B.C.** 1900—Abraham; 1720—Joseph and brothers in Egypt; 1250—Moses and the Exodus; 1000—David; 922—Divided kingdoms; 721—Fall of northern kingdom to Assyria; 587—Fall of southern kingdom to Babylon; 539—Exiles return; 515—Temple rebuilt; 445—Jerusalem's walls rebuilt; 332—Alexander the Great conquers Palestine; 167—Syrian persecution and Maccabee revolt; 142—Independence for Judea; 63—Romans conquer Jerusalem; 37—Herod the Great; 6—Birth of Jesus Christ.

**A.D.** 26—Jesus begins preaching; 30—Crucifixion and Resurrection of Jesus.

Most Bibles have maps of lands inhabited by the Jewish people. Try to become familiar with these lands. Note that at different times the Jewish homeland was known as the Promised Land, Canaan, Israel, Judah, Judea, Palestine, and the Holy Land.

*We should pray daily the prayer Jesus gave us:*

### *Our Father (Lord's Prayer)*

Our Father, who art in heaven, hallowed be thy name; thy kingdom come; thy will be done on earth as it is in heaven. Give us this day our daily bread; and forgive us our trespasses as we forgive those who trespass against us; and lead us not into temptation, but deliver us from evil. Amen.

# CHAPTER THREE
## Jesus Enters Our Tradition

The Jews who lived in Palestine during the last years of the reign of King Herod the Great (37-4 B.C.) hoped for better things. Senior citizens could remember how the Roman general Pompey had conquered Jerusalem in 63 B.C. The glory days of David were almost a thousand years in the past. People wondered, as they worshiped in the beautiful temple built by Herod, if there would ever be another David, as the prophets had foretold.

While the Jews were proud of their new temple, most of them resented Herod. He was a puppet of Rome, a master of intrigue, ruthless in putting down opposition. The situation in Palestine was tense, and there seemed to be little chance of getting rid of Herod or the Romans.

Some Jews in positions of wealth and power had adjusted to the presence of the Romans and cooperated with them. They were the *Sadducees*. Most of them were in the priestly class; they followed only the Torah, the written law. They did not believe in life after death, and their hopes were that peace and prosperity might prevail in this life. Other Jews expected God to send the Messiah as a military leader to conquer the Romans. These were the *Zealots*. Still others neither collaborated with the Romans nor fought against them. They centered their lives on observing the written law and thousands of other detailed prescriptions handed down as oral tradition. They believed in eternal life and hoped for a heavenly reward. These were the *Pharisees*. There were those who looked for peace in the desert, forming communities that practiced elaborate rituals. They hoped that their devotion would call down a Messiah who would lead them to heavenly glory. These were the *Essenes*.

The common people must have been influenced to some degree by all these groups. They met in their synagogues to hear the Scriptures and must have wondered how prophecies of a conquering Messiah could be reconciled with those of a Suffering Servant. How could Psalm 72:8 talk about a victorious Messiah who would "rule from sea to sea," and Isaiah 53:5 speak of this same person as being "pierced for our offenses, crushed for our sins"?

They pondered what Jeremiah could have meant when he said, "The days are coming, says the LORD, when I will make a new covenant with the house of Israel and the house of Judah" (Jeremiah 31:31). No one could have imagined the answer which lay hidden in the mind of God and that was about to unfold.

## The New Covenant (C 484–534)

God had plans that far surpassed human hopes. God knew what no one could imagine, that the new covenant would change the course of history because God would become a member of the human family.

And so, toward the end of King Herod's reign, God sent the angel Gabriel to Mary, a young woman of Nazareth in Galilee in the northern part of Palestine. Gabriel announced that Mary, engaged to a carpenter named Joseph, would have a child, the Son of God, by the power of the Holy Spirit. When Mary consented, "the Word became flesh and made his dwelling among us" (John 1:14). Mary soon left to visit her relatives Elizabeth and Zechariah who were expecting a child, though Elizabeth seemed past her childbearing years. Three months later Mary returned to Nazareth. When Joseph discovered that she was pregnant, he decided to end the engagement quietly. But an angel explained that Mary had conceived her Child by the Holy Spirit, and Joseph took Mary as his wife.

Shortly thereafter they had to go to Bethlehem to register for a census mandated by the Roman emperor. While they were there, Mary gave birth to her Son, named Jesus at his circumcision. When Jesus was presented at the Temple in Jerusalem, he was recognized as the Messiah by two elderly Jews, Simeon and Anna. He was honored with gifts by the magi from the East who had followed a star to his birthplace. Herod learned of Jesus' birth through the magi and tried to get information on his whereabouts. But the magi, warned in a dream that Herod actually wanted to kill the

Child, returned home secretly. Herod, in a rage, ordered the execution of all male boys two years old and under in the vicinity of Bethlehem. Mary and Joseph escaped the massacre by fleeing to Egypt, where they remained until Herod died. They then settled in Nazareth, where their life was so ordinary that the only thing reported was a pilgrimage to Jerusalem when Jesus was twelve years old. Left behind by Mary and Joseph when they departed from Jerusalem, he was found in the Temple, his "Father's house."

The infancy narratives of the Gospels of Matthew and Luke are meant to convey what is beyond history, that God became human in Jesus Christ. They hint that in the person of Jesus the Old Covenant was being transformed into the New. They cover the next eighteen years of his life by stating only that he "advanced [in] wisdom and age and favor before God and man" (Luke 2:52).

## The Kingdom of God Is at Hand (C 535–42, 551–53)

When Jesus was about thirty years old (Luke 3:23), his relative John, son of Elizabeth and Zechariah, began to preach at the Jordan River. Huge crowds flocked to hear his call to "prepare the way of the Lord" (Mark 1:3) and to be baptized as a sign of repentance. It was now time for Jesus to begin his mission. He went to John for baptism. John objected that he himself should be baptized by Jesus, then complied at Jesus' insistence. As Jesus came out of the water, the Spirit descended on him in the form of a dove, and a voice from heaven called out, "You are my beloved Son; with you I am well pleased" (Mark 1:11).

Jesus then withdrew into the Judean wilderness for forty days of fasting and prayer. As a human, Jesus needed to seek out his Father's way of bringing about his kingdom. The gospels tell us that Jesus was tempted by Satan to choose other ways, perhaps those of the Sadducees, Pharisees, and Zealots. The Sadducees were content with earthly comfort; Jesus was tempted to use his miraculous power to turn stones into bread for his own comfort. The Pharisees wanted to win favor by showy displays of holiness; Jesus was tempted to "win the crowds" by a spectacular leap from the Temple. The Zealots wanted a war-won kingdom; Jesus was tempted to accept all the kingdoms of the earth from Satan. Jesus resisted these temptations, went to Galilee, and began to teach.

Some time afterward, John the Baptizer was imprisoned by

Herod Antipas, son of Herod the Great and ruler of Galilee, because John had rebuked him for marrying his brother's wife. John had pointed out Jesus as the "Lamb of God" to his disciples, and some began to follow Jesus. From these and others Jesus formed a special group of Twelve Apostles (John 1:35-51; Matthew 4:18-22; 10:1-4).

## The Message of Jesus: His Parables (C 543–46)

Jesus began his preaching with the words: "This is the time of fulfillment. The kingdom of God is at hand. Repent, and believe in the gospel" (Mark 1:15). He painted colorful pictures in his parables, stories which illustrated important truths about God's kingdom and described it to his listeners.

1. The kingdom of God is present in Jesus. It is like a hidden treasure or a pearl of great price, of more value than anything (Matthew 13:44-46). To accept the kingdom is to build our lives on solid rock (Matthew 7:24-27). We accept it not by praising ourselves like the proud Pharisee but by seeking God's mercy like the humble tax collector (Luke 18:9-14). The seed of God's kingdom is God's word; we must be like fertile soil, well prepared to receive it (Matthew 13:1-23).

2. The gospel, the Good News, is that God wants to give mercy and forgiveness to all. God loves us with a gentle tenderness beyond our wildest dreams. God is like a shepherd who seeks the lost sheep, a woman who searches for a lost coin, a loving father who welcomes back his wayward son (Luke 15).

3. We cannot receive God's mercy unless we share it with others. We must not imitate the servant who sought mercy from his master, then denied it to a fellow servant (Matthew 18:23-35), or the rich man who let a beggar starve at his gate (Luke 16:19-31). Our model is the Good Samaritan, who cared for an unfortunate stranger (Luke 10:25-37). Our eternal destiny will depend on how we treat Christ who comes to us in the hungry, thirsty, and neglected (Matthew 25:31-46).

4. God is almighty, and the kingdom God establishes

through Jesus cannot be destroyed. No matter how much the kingdom is opposed, it will triumph. Just as a farmer is sure of the harvest even after an enemy has planted weeds in his wheat (Matthew 13:24-30,36-43), so God's kingdom cannot be snuffed out. As a mustard seed grows into a large shrub, so the seed of the Church planted by Christ will surely flourish (Matthew 13:31-32). As leaven placed in dough will make the whole loaf rise, so Christ's kingdom will have its effect on the world (Matthew 13:33).

5. All this calls for a response. With Jesus a decisive turning point in history has arrived. We must change our lives and put God's kingdom first. If we miss this opportunity, we are like a farmer who built huge barns to store his crops, only to die before he could enjoy their benefits (Luke 12:16-21); we are like foolish young women who are invited to a wedding but don't have oil for their lamps (Matthew 25:1-13). We are invited to the banquet of heaven, and Jesus urges us to accept the invitation (Matthew 22:1-14).

Thus the parables teach us that God offers us the kingdom—life and joy through Jesus. Now is the time to accept it, rejoice in it, and share it.

## The Message of Jesus:
## The Sermon on the Mount (C 543–44, 1716–29)

A good summary of the content and style of Jesus' teaching may be found in the Sermon on the Mount in chapters 5 through 7 of Matthew. The sermon begins with the beatitudes, in which Jesus turns the values of the secular world upside down: happy are they who place their trust in God and put God's kingdom first.

Jesus is not afraid to make serious moral demands: fidelity to God's law, victory over anger and lust, commitment in marriage, forgiveness, love of enemies, generosity. God has been generous to us. We must imitate God.

Jesus teaches us to pray to God as "our Father." In the Lord's Prayer we acknowledge the preeminence of God. We ask for the grace to do God's will and so help bring about God's kingdom. We place the present, past, and future in God's hands. We pray about our present needs (our "daily bread"), seek forgiveness for past misdeeds, and ask to be delivered from future trials.

Jesus teaches us to put God first—a god second to money or to anything else is not God. He assures us that God loves us and that we are of great value because we matter to the Maker of the universe.

Here in the Sermon on the Mount is a pattern for living that is psychologically and spiritually sound: healthy self-esteem, generous love for others, belief in God as origin and goal of life.

## The Message of Jesus:
## The Last Supper Discourse (C 2604, 2746–51)

In the Last Supper discourse of Jesus (John 14–17), Jesus reveals the inner life of God as Father, Son, and Holy Spirit. He invites his followers to share God's love. He offers us the closest possible intimacy with God. He encourages us to love one another with the love he has for us. He promises a peace that cannot be taken away. He assures us that nothing, not even death itself, can separate us from the life, love, joy, and peace he came to bring.

## The Miracles of Jesus (C 547–49)

Jesus' words alone would have been enough to gather huge audiences. But he also worked miracles, astounding signs that had no natural explanation and which attracted multitudes. Jesus healed. He gave sight to the blind and hearing to the deaf. He helped the lame to walk and the paralyzed to move. Jesus exercised power over nature. He changed water into wine to keep a wedding party going, and he multiplied bread and fish to feed a hungry crowd. He calmed the raging sea. Most remarkably, Jesus conquered death. He brought back to life the daughter of a Jewish official (Mark 5:21-43), a widow's son, (Luke 7:11-17), and his friend Lazarus (John 11:1-44).

Jesus worked these miracles because he wanted to bring God's love to people and to demonstrate the power of God (Mark 2:1-12). At times Jesus worked miracles in response to the faith of individuals (Matthew 8:5-13; Luke 8:43-48). At times there is no mention of faith in those he cured (Luke 7:11-17). He healed many, but surely there were many others he did not heal. There is no formula to explain miracles as they occurred during Jesus' ministry or as they occur today. Miracles are free actions of God, and we do not know why God works miracles in some cases and not in others. We accept them as signs of God's love and leave the mystery in God's hands.

### Jesus' Power Over Satan (C 328–36, 391–95, 550)

When Satan tried to tempt Jesus at the very beginning of his mission, Jesus resisted, and he continued to exercise authority over the devil. The gospels tell how Jesus drove evil spirits from people (Mark 1:23-28; Matthew 8:28-34) and state that he did this on many other occasions (Mark 1:34,39).

The Bible takes the existence of good and evil spirits for granted. God has created spiritual beings called angels. Some of them have rebelled against God and are known as devils or demons. They are personified in the Scriptures as Satan, Lucifer, or Beelzebul. Throughout human history, demons have tried to get people to join in their rebellion. The refusal of demons and of human beings to obey God is sin, source of all evil.

Jesus' power over demons is another sign that the kingdom of God is present in him (Matthew 12:28). God does not annihilate creatures when they misuse their freedom, and so demons continue to exist. But Jesus brings victory over Satan, and he gives others the power to conquer Satan (Luke 10:17-20).

### The Response to Jesus (C 554–94)

Jesus preached the Good News that God wants to fulfill our fondest hopes for life, joy, and peace. He worked miracles that revealed God's presence, mercy, and power. He demonstrated mastery over evil. We might expect, then, that all would have accepted him as Savior. Such was not the case.

It is true that large crowds flocked to Jesus, but they were looking for a Savior who would establish an earthly kingdom, and Jesus had to resist their attempts to proclaim him king (John 6:15). At times he commanded people not to say anything about his miracles (Mark 1:40-45; Mark 5:40-43). He had to correct even his own apostles for seeking a worldly kingdom (Matthew 20:20-28).

Jesus' popularity alarmed the Sadducees, who were afraid that the large crowds might start a civil war which would end in the destruction of Israel (John 11:45-54). The Zealots certainly noticed the large crowds, and no doubt they had hopes of recruiting Jesus and his followers, more so because one of the Twelve

Apostles seems to have been a member of the Zealot party (Luke 6:15).

While the Sadducees feared that Jesus might cause a civil disturbance, the Pharisees were enraged by the content of his teaching. Jesus refused to sanction their practice of keeping thousands of detailed regulations. The Pharisees and scribes (specialists in Jewish law) accused Jesus of breaking the law and criticized him for speaking with sinners. They accused him of driving out demons by the power of Satan. In time they allied themselves with Sadducees and Herodians (supporters of King Herod Antipas) and began to plot against Jesus (Mark 3:6).

So Jesus was faced with huge crowds of people who misunderstood his message, with the wealthy and powerful who feared him, with subversives who hoped to use him to their advantage, and with the religiously influential who opposed his teaching. The wonder is that Jesus continued to preach! He realized that his enemies were growing stronger in their resolve to destroy him, but he had come to bring God's mercy to all, even his enemies. He refused to use his miraculous power to crush his foes, relying only on love to call them to repentance. They refused to respond, and Jesus began to tell his apostles that he would be delivered into the hands of his foes.

Finally, Jesus decided to go to Jerusalem to face his enemies in their own stronghold. He went at Passover time when the population of Jerusalem, normally less than one hundred thousand, was multiplied many times by pilgrims. Accompanied by throngs of followers, Jesus rode into the city on a donkey, not a war-horse, to show that he was not interested in an earthly kingdom. There he confronted his enemies directly. He drove from the Temple those who were changing money and marketing animals for sacrifices, extorting huge profits from the poor (Luke 19:45-48); he thereby angered the priests and Sadducees who benefited from those profits. He denounced the Pharisees, apparently in a last attempt to shock them into recognizing their hardness of heart (Matthew 23). But they, along with the Sadducees and Herodians, only intensified their efforts to have Jesus killed.

## The Crucifixion and Death of Jesus (C 595–98)

Because of Jesus' popularity with the multitudes of pilgrims, the Sadducees, Herodians, and Pharisees could not risk arresting

Jesus publicly. Then Judas Iscariot, one of Jesus' apostles, went to the chief priests and offered to betray Jesus for thirty pieces of silver. On Thursday evening after Jesus had shared the Last Supper with his apostles, he went with them to pray in a garden called Gethsemane on the Mount of Olives outside the city walls. Soldiers led by Judas arrested Jesus, who was abandoned by his apostles, and took him to the chief priests. He was questioned, subjected to an unfair trial, and sentenced to death.

But because the Jewish leaders did not want to be blamed for Jesus' death, and because they wanted him to undergo the humiliation of a Roman crucifixion, they led him to the Roman governor, Pontius Pilate, and accused him of treason. Pilate questioned Jesus and decided that he was innocent. After sending him to Herod Antipas, in Jerusalem for the Passover, he had Jesus scourged to placate the Jewish leaders. He then tried to release Jesus, but the chief priests gathered a mob to shout for Jesus' execution. Finally, Pilate gave in and condemned Jesus to death.

Jesus was led to a place outside the city walls called Golgotha. There he was crucified between two criminals. He suffered the horrors of crucifixion for at least three hours. In his agony, he showed concern for his Mother, who was there at the cross with one beloved disciple and a few faithful women. He promised heaven to one of the criminals who turned to him as Lord. He forgave those who had crucified him. He commended his spirit to his heavenly Father and died. A Roman soldier thrust a spear into his side to guarantee the fact of his death.

Joseph of Arimathea, an admirer of Jesus, asked Pilate for his body. Aided by Nicodemus, he placed the body of Jesus in a tomb and covered its entrance with a huge stone. The chief priests and Pharisees, having heard of Jesus' statement that he would rise from the dead, went to Pilate and asked for soldiers to guard the tomb to keep his apostles from taking the body. This was done, and a seal was placed on the stone blocking the entrance. Jesus' enemies felt that they were rid of him once and for all.

### Why the Crucifixion? (C 599–623)

Why did Christ die on the cross? Scripture says that it was to free us from the bonds of sin, to redeem us (Romans 5:1-11). Sin had created a chasm between us and God that we could never bridge. Mere created beings could not atone for the insult of sin against their Creator. The bond of friendship between people and God could be restored only if God took the initiative. God did that in the Incarnation. By becoming one of us, Jesus Christ brought us God's perfect love.

But God's love is a threat to evil, and evil always lashes out against it. By becoming human, Jesus made himself vulnerable, liable to suffering and death. Evil attacked Jesus when his enemies decided that he must be killed.

This would happen in any age. If Jesus came to earth today and went to a troubled spot, asking enemies to love one another, he would quickly be eliminated. Once Jesus became one of us, it was just a matter of time until he would be murdered. He knew and accepted this. He came armed only with love, completely vulnerable to his enemies, "like a lamb led to the slaughter" (Isaiah 53:7).

Nothing but God's love could save us. Jesus' death on the cross was the greatest act of God's love in the history of the universe, and it brought us salvation. "No one has greater love than this, to lay down one's life for one's friends" (John 15:13). "God proves his love for us in that while we were still sinners Christ died for us" (Romans 5:8). Thus "we were reconciled to God through the death of his Son" (Romans 5:10).

## The Resurrection (C 624–58)

Jesus had been crucified on a Friday. The burial arranged by his friends was hastily done before the Sabbath rest. On the third day after his death, some women went to the tomb to anoint his body with spices. They were astonished to find the stone rolled back and the tomb empty; they ran to tell his apostles, who were in hiding. No one knew what to make of the empty tomb until Jesus appeared to his followers risen and glorious, no longer limited by time or space.

For a period of forty days, Jesus appeared often to his apostles and to others. The gospel narratives of the Resurrection (Matthew 28; Mark 16; Luke 24; John 20-21) show that Jesus' followers were certain that he had risen. The faith of the early Church is expressed by the reluctant believer, Thomas, who fell on his knees before Jesus and said, "My Lord and my God!" (John 20:28).

At first the Resurrection of Jesus had seemed to the apostles too good to be true. Then they realized that it was true and too good to hide. The very apostles who had abandoned Jesus at his arrest now began fearlessly to proclaim him as the Savior foretold in Old Testament prophecies. In the face of determined opposition and persecution, they preached that Jesus had come to bring salvation to all. The risen Jesus "worked with them and confirmed the word through accompanying signs" (Mark 16:20).

### *Questions for Discussion or Reflection*

Is Jesus real to you? Do you talk to him as you talk to other friends? Do you feel comfortable talking about Jesus with others? Do you realize that Jesus is truly closer to you and more present to you now than he would have been if you had lived in Palestine two thousand years ago?

The crucifix is an image of Christ hanging on the cross. Many Catholics place a crucifix in a prominent place in their homes. Look up 1 Corinthians 1:23 and 2:2. Do these passages help explain the importance of the crucifix to Catholics? Do you have a crucifix in your home?

### *Activities*

Write down in your own words answers to these questions: "Who is Jesus Christ?" "What are the most important elements of Jesus' message?"

Read John 1:35-42. Hear Jesus inviting you to spend some time with him. Remember that Jesus is with you as you pray, and enjoy being with him.

Read John 20:24-29. Kneel and speak the words of Thomas to Jesus, "My Lord and my God!" Hear Jesus saying to you, "Blessed are those who have not seen and have believed." Ask Jesus to strengthen your faith in him.

The Church has expressed its faith in Jesus Christ for centuries in the prayer called the Apostles' Creed, so named because it reflects the teaching of the apostles. You may wish to memorize this prayer.

### *Apostles' Creed*

I believe in God, the Father almighty, creator of heaven and earth. I believe in Jesus Christ, his only Son, our Lord. He was conceived by the power of the Holy Spirit and born of the Virgin Mary. He suffered under Pontius Pilate, was crucified, died, and was buried. He descended to the dead. On the third day he rose again. He ascended into heaven, and is seated at the right hand of the Father. He will come again to judge the living and the dead. I believe in the Holy Spirit, the holy catholic Church, the communion of saints, the forgiveness of sins, the resurrection of the body, and the life everlasting. Amen.

# CHAPTER FOUR
## Jesus in His Followers
## and in His Word

"All power in heaven and on earth has been given to me. Go, therefore, and make disciples of all nations, baptizing them in the name of the Father, and of the Son, and of the holy Spirit, teaching them to observe all that I have commanded you. And behold, I am with you always, until the end of the age" (Matthew 28:18-20). With these words the risen Jesus commissioned his disciples and assured them of his continuing presence. Jesus then ascended to heaven on a cloud (Acts 1:9) to God's right hand (Mark 16:19).

Jesus promised to be with his followers, then departed. How could this be? The cloud, the ascension, and the expression "at God's right hand" are meant to show that Jesus is truly "Lord and God," no longer limited by space or time. Jesus was not taken away; he is where God is—everywhere (C 659-67).

### The Coming of the Holy Spirit (C 731–36)

After the Ascension, the apostles returned to Jerusalem and gathered in an upper room with Mary, the Mother of Jesus, and with other believers. They prayed. They chose Matthias to replace Judas Iscariot, who had committed suicide after betraying Jesus (Acts 1:13-26). They must have discussed over and over again the incredible things that had happened since they had first met Jesus. They must have wondered how they, such a tiny group of uneducated people, could possibly "make disciples of all nations."

Their waiting ended and any misgivings vanished in a mysterious outpouring of courage and wisdom, which Luke describes as a strong driving wind and tongues of fire. "They were all filled with the holy Spirit" (Acts 2:4). Led by Peter, the apostles left their upper room and began to preach to the crowds assembled in Jerusalem for the feast of Pentecost.

Peter announced that Jesus was the fulfillment of Old Testament prophecies and had been raised from the dead as Lord and Messiah. He invited his listeners to repent and be baptized in the name of Jesus for the forgiveness of their sins, and promised that they, too, would receive the Holy Spirit. Three thousand were baptized on that day, and as the apostles continued to preach, more and more people put their faith in Jesus (Acts 2:14-47).

When Peter and John healed a crippled beggar, the Jewish authorities arrested them and threatened punishment if they continued to preach in Jesus' name. Peter and John responded, "Whether it is right in the sight of God for us to obey you rather than God, you be the judges. It is impossible for us not to speak about what we have seen and heard" (Acts 4:19-20).

As the apostles continued to proclaim Jesus as Messiah and Lord, the number of believers grew, and so did the opposition to them. A deacon named Stephen was executed. Saul, the overseer of this murder, "was trying to destroy the church; entering house after house and dragging out men and women, he handed them over for imprisonment" (Acts 8:3). It was about A.D. 36, five or six years after Christ's Resurrection. (All dates are A.D. unless otherwise noted.)

Then came a dramatic and unexpected development. Saul, on his way from Jerusalem to Damascus to arrest followers of Jesus, had a vision of the risen Christ. He became a believer and began to proclaim Jesus as the Messiah. Soon the persecutor became the persecuted and when some Jews tried to kill him, he escaped and spent the next few years in Tarsus and Arabia (Acts 9).

### The Spread of the Gospel (C 737–47)

Meantime, the believers began to preach the gospel to Jews and Gentiles alike. They made converts in towns south of Jerusalem, like Gaza, and moved west and north along the Mediterranean coast to Lydda, Joppa, Caesarea, Tarsus (Saul's hometown), and Antioch, where they were first called "Christians" (Acts 10–11).

Another persecution broke out in 44, this one started by Herod Agrippa, grandson of Herod the Great and ruler of Judea from 41 to 44. He killed James, the son of Zebedee, and arrested other Christians, including Peter, who miraculously escaped from prison (Acts 12). In spite of such troubles Christians continued to preach, grow in number, and care for one another. Christians at Antioch, for example, sent relief aid to famine-stricken believers in Judea (Acts 12). Such instances of concern united Christians. At the same time they were gradually moving away from their Jewish ties because of the persecutions against them and because so many Jews refused to accept Jesus as the Savior.

After Herod's death in 44, Saul (now known as Paul) and Barnabas (another early missionary) were sent by the Church at Antioch to preach the gospel in Cyprus and Asia Minor. They first spoke in Jewish synagogues but met with much hostility and persecution. They then turned to the Gentiles (non-Jews) and brought many people to Christ (Acts 13–14).

Some Christians of Jewish background, however, objected because Paul and Barnabas received converts without requiring them to observe Jewish law. These Christians stated that believers must observe all Old Testament regulations, but their opinion was rejected by Church leaders at a council in Jerusalem in 49. The crucial argument was given by Peter: "We believe that we are saved through the grace of the Lord Jesus" (Acts 15:11).

The Jerusalem council illustrated a profound truth. Jesus Christ is the Word of God and the revelation of God; any other word or revelation must be judged in the light of Jesus' life and teaching. Salvation can be found only in Christ. Christians now clearly recognized this as the foundation of their tradition, and henceforth the Old Testament would be judged in the light of the New. Christianity was no longer seen as a Jewish sect, but as a religion for all people—a "catholic" religion.

Christianity soon spread throughout the civilized world. The Acts of the Apostles focuses on Paul, telling how he brought the gospel to many parts of Asia Minor and Europe, including the very heart of the Roman Empire, Rome itself. Other missionaries took the gospel to Africa, India, and Asia, their task made easier by Roman roads and by the Roman peace.

But Rome soon became a foe. The Emperor Nero instigated a persecution against the Christians in the mid sixties and, according to tradition, both Peter and Paul were martyred in Rome at this time. By every logic, the mighty Roman Empire should have crushed Christianity, but the "blood of martyrs is the seed of Christians," and the Church continued to grow.

Rome played a major part in another development. After the death of Herod Agrippa in 44, the Zealots pressed for a "holy war" against the Romans. In 66 the unrest exploded into a full-blown revolt. In 70 the Romans besieged Jerusalem, slaughtered its inhabitants, and reduced the city to ruins. The Temple was no more, and Christianity was separated even further from its Jewish roots.

## Formation of the New Testament and Christian Bible (C 120)

For twenty years after the Resurrection of Christ, missionaries spread the Good News of Jesus by preaching. Eventually, Christians began to feel a need to preserve their heritage in writing. Collections of the sayings of Jesus, liturgical prayers, and professions of faith began to appear. In 51 or 52 Paul started to write letters to the towns and cities he had evangelized. These letters were preserved and shared and soon were recognized as having a special authority. By 65 or 70 the Gospel of Mark was written. Other gospels and writings followed. Some were accepted by the Church as inspired, while others were rejected. At the same time books regarded by Jews as inspired were evaluated by Christians, and gradually a list or "canon" of books was compiled.

The process by which the Catholic Church came to accept the Bible as we have it today is a long and complex one. At the time of Christ, there were different opinions among Jews about which books should be accepted as divinely inspired. While there were probably no definitive lists until well after the time of Christ, there were two popular collections. One of these collections, the Palestinian, was written in Hebrew. The other, the Alexandrian (or Septuagint), included a Greek translation of the Hebrew books and a number of books written in Greek. The Palestinian and Alexandrian collections were honored by different Jewish communities, but because the New Testament authors wrote in Greek, they tended to use the Alexandrian collection, and it soon became the accepted "Old Testament" of the Christian community. The Palestinian collection was later chosen by a group of Jewish scholars as their sacred book about 100, partially in reaction against the Christian use of the Alexandrian collection.

By 125 many writings about Jesus, including all of those now found in the New Testament, were being circulated among Christians. Some of the writings were regarded as authoritative because of their apostolic origins and doctrinal content. Some were rejected because they contained false teachings. Gradually, the Christian community began to regard certain writings as inspired by God. By the end of the fourth century there was general consensus that the Christian Bible should contain the forty-six books of the Alexandrian Old Testament and the twenty-seven books of the New Testament now found in the Catholic Bible. Such consensus was reflected in lists of biblical books drawn up in the Church councils of Hippo in 393 and of Carthage in 397.

There was little disagreement among Christians until the sixteenth century, when Protestants rejected the Alexandrian (Christian) list of Old Testament books in favor of the Palestinian (Jewish) list. In 1546 the Council of Trent defined the Alexandrian as the official list of Old Testament books for Catholics. As a result the Protestant Old Testament contains seven fewer books than the Catholic: Tobit, Judith, First and Second Maccabees, Wisdom, Sirach (sometimes called Ecclesiasticus), and Baruch (plus additions to Esther and Daniel). These books are placed in some Protestant Bibles as the "Apocrypha."

After breaking from the Catholic Church, Martin Luther relegated Hebrews, James, Jude, and Revelation to a secondary position in the New Testament. Other Protestants maintained the traditional New Testament list, and today all Protestant churches accept the same twenty-seven books as does the Catholic Church. We move now to a "global view" of these books.

### The Gospels (C 124–27)

No books have touched the hearts and lives of people so dramatically as have the four gospels. Through the gospels we are put in touch with Jesus himself, we hear the preaching of the early apostles, and we read the words of the evangelists who gave us the gospels in their present form.

The gospels were not produced immediately after the Resurrection of Jesus. The *Catechism of the Catholic Church* notes three stages in their development. The first stage was the life and teaching of Jesus. The second was the oral preaching of Jesus' followers and the earliest writings about him. The third stage was the work of the gospel writers, the evangelists, which consisted in collecting materials about Jesus and adapting them to meet the needs of specific audiences.

*Matthew*, the first gospel in our present New Testament arrangement of books, was written after Mark, and most likely used Mark as a source. The book is named after the apostle Matthew, but its actual author is unknown. He wrote around the year 80 and probably intended his gospel for Jewish Christians. In many ways the gospel shows that Jesus is the fulfillment of Old Testament prophecy, and the main body of the gospel is divided into five sections, which would remind Jews of the Pentateuch.

*Mark* was written in 65 or 70, probably for non-Jewish Christians. It is the shortest of the gospels, and presents Jesus as the suffering Messiah who was misunderstood and rejected until his Resurrection. Many think that the author is John Mark, a missionary who traveled with Paul and had some contact with Peter.

*Luke* appeared about the same time as Matthew and probably used Mark as a source also. Luke was a skilled Greek author who addressed his gospel and its companion volume, the Acts of the Apostles, to Greek-speaking Christians. The author is usually identified as a missionary who traveled with Paul. He emphasizes the mercy and forgiveness of Jesus, as well as the joy his salvation brings. For Luke, Christ's life was a "journey to Jerusalem," to suffering and death and glory.

*John* was written ten or more years after Luke and differs from the other three gospels in language and style. The author has been identified as the apostle John, or one of his disciples, but this is uncertain. The gospel may have been written for Christians around Ephesus in Asia Minor. Rich in symbolism, it reflects upon the life and teachings of Jesus as he lives in the Church and the sacraments.

## Acts, Letters, and Revelation

The *Acts of the Apostles* takes up where the Gospel of Luke leaves off. Written by the same author and at the same time as the Gospel of Luke, Acts describes the beginnings of the Church in Jerusalem (chapters 1–5), the first missions outside Jerusalem and the conversion of Paul (6–12), the missionary journeys of Paul (13–21), and Paul's arrest and trip to Rome (21–28). Acts gives us a unique view of the early Church and its preaching.

The next twenty-one books of the New Testament are called

"letters." Some can properly be called letters in our modern sense, but others are actually sermons or theological treatises. They include the earliest and latest writings of the New Testament. Thirteen are attributed to Paul. However, Paul dictated many of his letters to secretaries, and others may have been composed by fellow workers who depended on outlines or basic themes drawn up by Paul. Some of the letters attributed to Paul or other New Testament leaders may have been composed after their deaths by writers who used ideas originating with Paul and the other leaders.

None of the letters is a complete theological explanation of Christian doctrine. They were written to meet specific needs of the early Christians to solve problems as they arose. They represent increasing insight into the meaning of Christ's life and message as gained by the apostles and early Christians under the guidance of the Holy Spirit. Since many of the problems encountered are the same as those we face today, the letters speak to us, giving insights into the life of the early Church and addressing God's Word to us.

*Romans*, written by Paul in about 58, is a strongly reasoned argument that we are saved by faith in Jesus Christ, not by observance of Old Testament law. Paul devotes the last four chapters to an explanation of the moral duties of Christians and to the meaning of life in Christ.

*First* and *Second Corinthians* were written between 54 and 58. Corinth was a Greek city known for its loose morals, and the Christians of Corinth needed a great deal of encouragement and correction from Paul after their conversion from paganism. In these letters Paul addresses issues like cliques in the community, sexual morality, virginity and marriage, eucharistic assemblies, charismatic gifts, love, and the Resurrection.

*Galatians* was written by Paul in about 54 to believers in Galatia (modern Turkey). Paul refutes those who demanded that Christians be circumcised, and he reminds believers that we are saved by faith in Christ.

*Ephesians* may have been written by a follower of Paul about 90, well after Paul's death. It is addressed to the Christian community in Ephesus (a seaport in Turkey). It proclaims the uniqueness of Christ as Son of God and the oneness of the Church with Christ, and it lays the foundation for our understanding of the Church as "one, holy, catholic, and apostolic."

*Philippians* is a beautiful document that may contain parts of three letters sent by Paul to converts at Philippi, a city in northern Greece. Paul thanks the Philippians for their generous assistance, assures them of his love for them, and exhorts them to remain one in Jesus the Lord.

*Colossians* proclaims Jesus as Son of God and Head of his Body, the Church, echoing many of the ideas of Ephesians. It encourages Christians to die to sinful ways and to live in union with the risen Savior. Addressed to the community of Colossae, a small town in southwestern Turkey, it may well be a sermon written after Paul's death, using Paul as a "heavenly spokesman."

*First Thessalonians* is the oldest book in the New Testament. Written by Paul in about 51 to the Church at Thessalonica, a seaport in northern Greece, it reminds the Christians of Paul's loving mission to them and encourages them to be faithful as they await the coming of Christ, which they apparently expected in their lifetime. *Second Thessalonians* was written later to answer more questions about the coming of Christ.

*First* and *Second Timothy* and *Titus* are called the "pastoral letters" because they are addressed to early Church leaders as guides for the pastoral care of their communities. They may have been written after Paul's death by inspired authors who wanted to offer guidance to Christians around the year 100 in the words of Paul. The letters reflect the growth of the Church and emphasize the importance of faithfulness to the gospel and to the teaching of the apostles.

*Philemon* is a personal letter written by Paul in 58 asking Philemon, an influential friend, to take back a runaway slave whom Paul had converted.

*Hebrews* is a carefully composed sermon whose author is unknown. Probably written late in the first century to Christians in general, it presents Christ as the Word of God, as Priest who saves us by his death, and as Leader who opens heaven to us.

*James* is the title of the next letter, but Scripture scholars debate about who James really is. The book is a sermon of the late first century, teaching that a living faith must show itself in good works and a holy life.

*First* and *Second Peter* are probably sermons written in Peter's name to encourage Christians of the late first century. The first letter uses baptismal liturgies, hymns, and other sources, including perhaps Peter's sermons, to comfort and encourage persecuted Christians. The second exhorts believers to remain faithful to Christ and always to be ready for his coming.

*First*, *Second*, and *Third John* are commonly believed to have come from the same Christian community that produced the Gospel of John. They were written late in the first century. First John proclaims Jesus as Son of God but also truly human; God is love, and therefore we are to love one another. Second John urges believers to remain faithful to Jesus. Third John is a short note requesting aid and hospitality for missionaries.

*Jude* is a short sermon written about 100, warning Christians to avoid false teachers and remain faithful to the teaching of the apostles. Much of Jude's message is found in chapter two of Second Peter.

*Revelation* belongs to that category of literature called "apocalypse," popular two hundred years before and after Christ. This literature uses figurative language, symbols and numbers, visions, heavenly messengers, and picturesque descriptions of the struggle between good and evil. The author of Revelation calls himself John (1:1,4,9), but we do not know just who this John is. The book may have been written in Ephesus to give encouragement to Christians of Asia Minor during times of persecution by the Roman Emperor Domitian (81–96). Many people have tried to use Revelation as a "heavenly timetable" to determine the end of the world, but Revelation was not intended for this. Indeed, our best way of understanding it may be to see it as a biblical *Star Wars*, that is, as an epic presentation of the battle between good and evil. As in the *Star Wars* movies, good is threatened as all kinds of monsters are unleashed by the forces of evil, but these are vanquished. Seen in this way, Revelation is a powerful statement that God will prevail over Satan. It says at the end of the Bible what Genesis states at the beginning: God is good, and God created the world good. Evil has entered the world because of sin, but God will overcome it. All people are called to be faithful to God in order to share in Christ's great triumph and heavenly joy.

### Biblical Inspiration: God Speaks to Us (C 128–41)

The Bible has been a "bestseller" for two thousand years. It addresses every human situation, reflects every emotion, paints vivid pictures of all kinds of people—good and bad. But the most important reason why the Bible is a bestseller is that it is inspired by God: God speaks to human beings through its pages. "All scripture is inspired by God" (2 Timothy 3:16; see Hebrews 4:12 and 2 Peter 1:19-21).

*Inspiration* as applied to the books of the Bible, means that God guided the human authors to write in such a way that the books teach the religious truth that God intended. This does not mean that the writers "took dictation" from God. Rather, they were touched in various ways by God to record God's presence and activity. Some may have been inspired in extraordinary visions, dreams, or angelic messengers. Others may have received inspiration through ordinary kinds of prayer or by recognizing God in events and circumstances. New Testament writers also experienced God through the words and actions of Jesus. In these ways, and in many others, God inspired the biblical authors, and they expressed what they experienced in the Bible.

When we pick up the Bible, because God is not limited by space or time, God speaks to us through the same words as those addressed to Moses, to David, to the prophets. When we pick up the Bible, Jesus speaks to us here and now just as he spoke to the apostles.

People of faith realize this unique aspect of the Bible, and all Christians should understand that when we open the Bible, we "dial God's number." We can take any other book from a library shelf, read it, and learn valuable information. All the while, the book's author is not aware of what we are doing. But when we pick up the Bible, God says, "Hello."

God's words are right there for us with answers to today's problems. "Indeed, the word of God is living and effective...and able to discern reflections and thoughts of the heart" (Hebrews 4:12). When we are discouraged, Jesus says to us, "Come to me, all you who labor and are burdened, and I will give you rest" (Matthew 11:28). When we are frightened, Jesus tells us, "Peace be with you" (John 20:19). When we are lonely, Jesus reminds us, "I am with you always" (Matthew 28:20).

When God speaks to us through the Bible, we are invited to respond. We respond through *prayer*: we read God's words, then talk to God as we would to any friend. We respond also through our *decisions*: we read until we come to a phrase that challenges us to make a change in our lives; then we make some practical decision based on what we have read. There is no other book that allows this kind of communication with God. Down through the centuries Christians who have understood this have revered the Bible as a sacred book, as a beloved companion, and as a treasured friend.

## The Bible, Sacred Tradition, and Revelation
## (C 74–100, 166–97)

By the end of the first century, most of the books of the New Testament had been written. By the end of the second century, most Christians accepted the forty-six books of the Old Testament and twenty-seven books of the New Testament. By the end of the fourth century, official lists of these seventy-three books were approved by Church councils.

By proclaiming these books to be inspired by God and by rejecting others as not inspired, the Church, guided by the Holy Spirit, was saying, "This is what we believe about God, about Jesus, about life and death, about what we are as a Church. And this is what we reject." The books of the Bible, in turn, helped shape the beliefs of each new generation of Christians.

All of this was a dynamic process involving some conflict. In the first four centuries after Christ, there were those who wanted to put limits on the saving action of Jesus by claiming that all Christians should follow the Law of Moses. There were those who said that Jesus was God, but not human; others said that Jesus was human, but not God. Some said that Jesus revealed God as Father, Son, and Holy Spirit; others denied this. The early Church expressed its beliefs about these and other matters in the biblical books it accepted as inspired, in the decisions of councils, in formulas of belief called creeds, and in its worship. As this happened, believers became the kind of Church which we recognize as "Catholic."

The process by which the Bible was formed can help us understand what the Catholic Church means by sacred Tradition. *Tradition* means "handing on," and sacred Tradition includes the way the Church has handed on and interpreted the Bible, as well as creeds, worship, decisions of councils, and the consistent teaching of the Church down through the centuries. These may not contradict the Bible but are based on the Bible and expand upon it.

The Bible and sacred Tradition comprise what the Church understands as divine revelation. Catholics do not think that our belief can be limited to the Bible alone because early in the life of the Church there was no New Testament! Further, sacred Tradition is necessary if the Church is to apply the teaching of the Bible to changing circumstances. We believe that the Church does this under the guidance of the Holy Spirit. Jesus said, "I have much more to tell you, but you cannot bear it now. But when he comes, the Spirit of truth, he will guide you to all truth" (John 16:12-13).

We have studied the books of the Bible. Now we turn to a study of what the Church proclaims as its belief about God, Jesus, and itself.

### *Questions for Discussion or Reflection*

Do you think that the Catholic Church could have come into being and that the New Testament could have been written if the Resurrection of Jesus were not a reality? What reasons could Peter and the apostles have possibly had to preach Jesus as Lord if he had not actually risen from the dead? If Jesus had not risen, can you imagine yourself as Peter trying to convince the apostles that they should pretend that Jesus was alive, even though the only things they stood to "gain" were persecution, suffering, and death? Does this strengthen your faith in the risen Christ?

"Jesus is more present to me today than he was to the apostles before he rose from the dead." "Jesus speaks to me today just as surely as he spoke to the apostles before his Resurrection." Are these statements true or false? Why?

### *Activities*

Open your Bible and page through the New Testament. Try to note the main categories of books and the length of the various books. Read a few of the introductions to the books. Look for passages you may be acquainted with and read some of them.

Pick up your Bible and ask the Holy Spirit to help you realize that you are "dialing God's number." Open your Bible to the Gospel of John and read chapter 17. Place yourself at the Last Supper with Jesus and his apostles. Listen to Jesus' prayer to his Father. When you get to verses 24 to 26, picture Jesus looking directly at you, speaking your name instead of "they" or "them."

# CHAPTER FIVE
## The Church—Jesus Unites Us to the Trinity

The first disciples of Christ believed that he had called them to proclaim his life, death, and resurrection (chapter three). They spread the gospel and began to identify certain writings as valid expressions of his life and teaching (chapter four). They had received a new vision of God from Jesus and began to recognize their unity with Christ in his Church. Their vision and their recognition can help us realize what it means to be "Church."

### The Trinity (C 198–267)

As Jews, the apostles believed in one God. But Jesus spoke to them of Father, Son, and Holy Spirit (John 14–17). Jesus was their "Lord and God" (John 20:28). Mysteriously, God was One, God was Three, and God was Jesus.

The disciples expressed their vision of God as Father, Son, and Holy Spirit in the New Testament. The life of Jesus began when Mary was overshadowed by the Holy Spirit and conceived the "Son of God" (Luke 1:35). As Jesus was baptized in the Jordan, the Father's voice was heard and the Spirit descended as a dove (Mark 1:10). The risen Jesus told his followers to baptize "in the name of the Father, and of the Son, and of the holy Spirit" (Matthew 28:19).

In time Church leaders began to speak of Father, Son, and Holy Spirit as the "Trinity." They chose formulas which expressed the Church's beliefs about the Trinity: there are "three Persons in one divine nature," the Son is "begotten" by the Father; the Holy Spirit "proceeds" from the Father and the Son. We use these formulas today when we recite the Nicene Creed at Mass.

The phrase "three Persons in one divine nature" expresses a mystery we cannot fully understand. But we can gain some insight into it. The word *person* refers to "who" we are. The word *nature* refers to "what" we are. If someone asks us, "Who are you?" we respond with our name…person. If someone asks us, "What are you?" we respond that we are human…our nature. With humans there is only one person in each human nature. But God is three divine Persons in one divine Nature (*divine* means "of God").

The word *begotten* is used in the Creed because it means that the Father and Son are of the same nature. When parents "beget" a child, they beget someone of the same nature as themselves. When people "make" something, they make something different. When we say that the Son is "begotten" by the Father, we profess our belief that the Son is equal to the Father, "true God from true God." When we say that the Holy Spirit "proceeds from the Father and the Son," we also express the equality of the Spirit with Father and Son.

Theologians have tried to offer insights into the Trinity by saying that the Father knows himself from all eternity, and this Knowledge is the Son. The Father and Son love each other with infinite love, and this Love is the Holy Spirit. I can know myself, and this idea, or mental picture, is real. I can love myself, and this love is real. But God's knowledge is so limitless that it is a Person, the Son. The love of Father and Son is so limitless that it, too, is a Person, the Holy Spirit.

Such insights may be helpful, but we can no more understand the inner life of God than a daisy can understand higher mathematics. We can realize, however, that Jesus revealed God as a Community of love because God wants to draw us into that Community. We are destined to spend eternity with the Trinity, and this "heaven" begins here on earth when we know God as Father, Son, and Holy Spirit.

## The Father (C 268–354)

God is Father. This does not mean that God is like human fathers, but that all good qualities in human parents come from God. The Bible tells us about these qualities. God cares and is close to us: "I will never forget you. See, upon the palms of my hands I have written your name" (Isaiah 49:15-16). God wants us to be free: as God freed the Israelites from slavery, so God frees us from sin (Deuteronomy 26:5-9). God forgives us our sins and wants us to experience God's forgiveness even more than we want to be forgiven (Luke 15). God loves us beyond imagining: "With age-old love I have loved you" (Jeremiah 31:3). God promises that good will win out over evil and that life will conquer death: "For I am convinced that neither death, nor life...will be able to separate us from the love of God" (Romans 8:38-39). To these qualities Jesus adds a special note of tenderness and affection when he addresses God as "Abba," equivalent to "Daddy" or "Dear Father" (Mark 14:36; Romans 8:15; Galatians 4:6).

God is Father-Creator. Some Christians say that Genesis teaches exactly *how* God created the world and that the Bible cannot be reconciled with scientific studies of the development of life forms and of the appearance of human beings on earth. But Catholics believe that the Bible teaches the *why* of creation, while science studies its *how.*

*Why* are we here? Because God exists and created us, and so life has meaning and we have hope for the future. *Why* is there right and wrong? Because God created us free and invites us to choose the right. *Why* is there such a thing as married love? Because God created us male and female to form marriage covenants modeled on God's faithfulness and love.

*How* did creation occur? According to a common scientific theory, creation began about fifteen billion years ago in an incredible explosion of power (the "big bang") which threw out all that now forms the universe. For Catholics, there is no necessary contradiction between such scientific theory and biblical teaching, as long as the scientific theory does not deny God's existence or the fact that all created things must come from God.

Because all created things come from God, we have a responsibility to care for them and to avoid any disordered use of things which would harm the environment. Because we are made in God's image and likeness, we must respect people of every race, nation, age, and creed.

### The Son (C 422–83)

God is Son. From all eternity, there is a relationship in God's being which we can best understand as "Father-Son." Then the New Testament teaches that the Son, the second Person of the Trinity, became human. "In the beginning was the Word, and the

Word was with God, and the Word was God....And the Word became flesh and made his dwelling among us" (John 1:1-14).

That God the Son became human is a miracle we call the Incarnation. It is a mystery completely beyond our comprehension, but false teachers have tried to bring the mystery down to our level. Some have denied that Jesus was truly human (2 John 7–9). Others have denied that he was truly God. The Catholic Church has always taught that Jesus is truly divine and truly human.

The Church explains that Jesus has a divine nature and a human nature, united in one divine Person, the "Word." We cannot understand how Jesus can be both God and a human being, but we believe it on the testimony of Scripture and of the Church. We believe it because Jesus worked miracles and because miracles still occur in his name. We believe it because Jesus rose from the dead, and in his victory over death, we see the presence of God. With Thomas the Apostle, every Catholic can say to Jesus, "My Lord and my God" (John 20:28).

It was, of course, through his human nature that his contemporaries made contact with Jesus, and it is still through his human nature that we encounter Jesus. Christ's human nature gives us our truest insights into the nature of God. Therefore, we should learn all we can about the human, Jesus.

What kind of a man was Jesus in his mortal life on earth? The Bible shows us that he was a real down-to-earth human being. Raised in a small town, he seemed such a normal child that when he came back as a teacher and miracle worker, people refused to believe he was special (Mark 6:1-6). At the age of twelve, he caused Mary and Joseph a great deal of anxiety when, without telling them, he stayed at the Jerusalem Temple instead of accompanying them back home (Luke 2:41-52). From his parables we can infer that Jesus observed life and loved nature: the sun and rain, wild flowers and vines and trees, moths and birds and foxes, people building houses, farmers planting crops, women baking bread, and fishermen casting their nets (Matthew 5–7; 13). He celebrated life (John 2:1-11). He was courageous yet experienced distress and sorrow (Mark 14:32-42). He was born like us and experienced death as we will (Luke 2:1-7; Luke 23).

Jesus liked people and people liked him. He was always getting invited to meals (Luke 4:39; 7:36; 10:38; 14:1). He enjoyed being with people (John 1:35-51). He cared about little children (Mark 10:13-16) and noticed people others missed (Mark 10:46-52). To him elderly widows and despised sinners were important (Mark 12:41-44; Mark 14:3-9).

Jesus was merciful and compassionate. He defended a woman accused of adultery (John 8:1-11). He shed tears at the death of Lazarus (John 11). He wept over the fate of Jerusalem (Luke 19:41-44).

Jesus was, and is, a friend. "No one has greater love than this, to lay down one's life for one's friends. You are my friends" (John 15:13-15).

This is the reality of the Incarnation: the kindness and mercy of Jesus, his concern for "little people," his love even to dying on the cross for us, his forgiveness of sinners, are the kindness, mercy, concern, love, and forgiveness of God. Jesus is Emmanuel, "God is with us" (Matthew 1:23)

## The Holy Spirit (C 683–730)

God is Holy Spirit. We Catholics believe that the Holy Spirit is the love eternally proceeding from the Father and Son. This does not mean "love" in an abstract sense, but "God who loves." The Holy Spirit, then, is the cause of all that is good and loving in the universe. If we want to know where the Holy Spirit is, we need only look for whatever is good and loving: the beauty of nature, the warmth of family life, the care people show one another.

The Holy Spirit is Love, and love is power, our source of strength as we follow Christ. Just as the Spirit descended as a dove upon Jesus at the beginning of his ministry (Matthew 3:16-17), so the Spirit descends upon us to guide us. The Holy Spirit is like the wind and fire which strengthened the apostles to witness for Christ (Acts 2:1-4). Wind is capable of moving huge ships across the water, but the ship must open its sails if it is to go anywhere. Fire can generate warmth and light, but it takes effort to utilize its energy.

Just so, we must "open our sails to the Spirit" to experience the power of God. We must open our hearts and lives to the warmth and light of the Spirit's fire. We do this by study of the Scriptures and by prayer and by humbly admitting our weakness to God. For the Holy Spirit works through our weakness and humanity, giving us strength to do what we could not otherwise accomplish. Hebrews 4:14-16 says that God sympathizes with our weakness and that we can confidently go to God for help in time of need. The apostles, ordinary people like us, touched by sin and failure, were able through the power of the Spirit to spread the faith throughout the world. The Spirit helped them; "the Spirit too comes to the aid of our weakness" (Romans 8:26), bringing us power, warmth, and light. So Jesus calls the Holy Spirit our "Advocate," our Helper, who guides us to the truth (John 14:15-18; 16:7-14).

## In God We Live and Move and Have Our Being (C 355–61, 1699–1715)

We human beings are made in such a way that we need to know and be known, love and be loved. Why is this? Because we exist in a "Trinitarian universe," designed by God's infinite Knowledge, created by God's infinite Love. We are made in the image and likeness of God (Genesis 1:27). Therefore, the Trinity is the most basic of our beliefs and the most practical. Our lives are "Trinitarian" because God is the Trinity.

We can make this realization a part of our lives each time we pray. In prayer we address God as the One from whom we come—the Father. We are aware of God at our side, teaching us to say "Our Father," standing with us as we pray—the Son. We are conscious of God within us, inspiring us to lift up our hearts, giving depth and feeling to our prayer—the Holy Spirit (Romans 8:14-17). In prayer we can picture God as our Father who gives all creatures life, Jesus as our Brother who walks alongside us, the Holy Spirit as the Guest of our souls. Through prayer we know Father, Son, and Spirit as our God, in whom "we live and move and have our being" (Acts 17:28).

## The Church, the Body of Christ (C 748–69)

We do not come before the Trinity as solitary human beings. Along with our inborn need to know and love God, we have a need to know and love other people and to be known and loved by them. Because we are made in the image and likeness of God, who is "Community," we need community.

Jesus came to draw us into the "Community love" of the Trinity. He lived, died, and rose to bring all people into one family (John 10:16-18). At the Last Supper, Jesus asked us to love one another as he loves us (John 15:12). He prayed that we would be one, as he and the Father are one (John 17:20-21).

He formed the community of believers into the sign of his continuing presence on earth. He said, "Where two or three are gathered together in my name, there am I in the midst of them" (Matthew 18:20). When Paul was persecuting Christians, Christ asked him, "Why are you persecuting me?" This helped Paul to understand the unity between Christ and believers. He later wrote to them, "You are Christ's body" (1 Corinthians 12:27), and explained that Christ "is the head of the body, the church" (Colossians 1:18).

Paul uses the terms *Body of Christ* and *church* interchangeably. The word *church* is a translation of the Greek word *ekklesia*, an assembly of people called forth, "the People of God." Christ calls forth believers to bring him to the world, especially by their love and community: "This is how all will know that you are my disciples, if you have love for one another" (John 13:35). It is the task of the Church, then, to perpetuate the love of Christ on earth and to mirror the love of the Trinity.

## The Imperfect Church:
## Christ's Beloved Church (C 770–80)

Since the Church is made up of human beings who are not perfect, it is to be expected that the Church will be less than perfect. Some people are scandalized by failures in the Church and say that Christ never intended a Church with its leaders, rituals, laws, and potential for scandal and sin.

But the first generation of Christians believed that Christ intended to establish a Church (Matthew 16:18) with leaders who would make decisions ratified by God: "Whatever you bind on earth shall be bound in heaven, and whatever you loose on earth shall be loosed in heaven" (Matthew 18:18). They believed that Christ gave them ritual observances by which to remember him: "This is my body, which will be given for you; do this in memory of me" (Luke 22:19). They accepted from Jesus strict rules of conduct (Matthew 6:21-22) and guidelines for marriage (Mark 10:11). They believed that Jesus expected his followers to have standards for membership in the Church, and that those who violated them were to be excluded: "If he refuses to listen even to the church, then treat him as you would a Gentile or a tax collector" (Matthew 18:17).

Jesus knew that those who would represent him were subject to failure. Peter denied him three times, but Jesus, after his Resurrection, gave Peter a threefold commission to care for his sheep (John 21:15-18). The apostles ran away when Jesus was arrested, and yet he appeared to them after his Resurrection and sent them to preach the gospel to all nations (Matthew 28:16-20). Jesus patiently helped the unbelieving Thomas to put faith in him (John 20:24-29).

The early Church had all the problems found in churches today. There were liars and hypocrites (Acts 5:1-11). There were complaints of unfairness (Acts 6:1). There were those who used religion for personal gain (Acts 8:9-24). There were disagreements about doctrine (Acts 15). There were conflicts among Church leaders (Acts 15:36-41). There were sermons that failed to make an impact upon the preacher's audience (Acts 17:22-34) and sermons so long that they put people to sleep (Acts 20:7-12). There were questions about pastors' salaries, disorder at worship ceremonies, lust and scandal, and neglect of the poor (1 Corinthians 5-11). There were all the problems which arise when people try to follow Jesus and fall short of the mark because of human weakness and sin.

Because the Church is the Body of Christ, it has never lacked goodness and grace. If there were villains in the early Church, there were also heroes (Acts 7). If there was sin, there was holiness (Acts 2:42-47). If there was selfishness, there was generosity (Acts 4:32-37). If there were laws and leaders, it was because no society can exist without them (Acts 6:1-7). If there were ritual ceremonies, it was because these were faithful responses to Christ's will (1 Corinthians 11:23-26). If there were times when the followers of Jesus failed him, there were also times when they were heroic in professing his gospel (Acts 4:1-22).

In the Church there have always been good and bad people, good and bad times. The history of the Church has been the history of Christ living in us, inviting us to follow him faithfully, and calling us back when we fail.

## Christ in the History of His Church (C 781–82)

If there had been such a thing as the "evening news" in the first century, the activities of the first Christian preachers would probably have not been reported. A tiny religious movement proclaiming that an executed man was alive would hardly have been thought important by the worldly wise. But as we read in the Acts of the

Apostles, those first preachers converted thousands to Christ, and communities of believers were established in many major cities of the Roman Empire. In a few years they came to the attention of the Emperor Nero, a madman who launched a bloody persecution of the Church in 64, killing Peter, Paul, and many innocent men, women, and children. Other persecutions followed, but Christianity continued to spread. There were about half a million believers by the year 100 and several million by 300. During this time patterns for Church structure were established, as local churches were led by bishops and assisted by priests and deacons. Disputes about the real nature of God and Christ led bishops to clarify the Church's beliefs in conciliar decrees and creeds.

In 313 the Church entered a new era. The Roman Emperor Constantine issued the decree of Milan, granting religious tolerance to Christians. Soon he began to support Christianity in various ways. This ended the persecutions, but it also opened a door to church-state entanglements that would create new problems for the Church. When the African priest Arius taught falsely that Jesus was not truly God, interference by emperors complicated the bishops' efforts to state the true belief of the Church. Eventually the teaching of the Councils of Nicea in 325 and Constantinople in 381 prevailed, and the Creed formulated by these Councils is still prayed by Catholics at Mass.

In the fifth century the Roman Empire began to collapse as barbarian tribes invaded its once secure boundaries. The Church became a civilizing force among these tribes as they were slowly converted to Christ. Monastic communities, which had been in existence for several hundred years, began to expand in the sixth century under Saint Benedict and were instrumental in the spread of the gospel. In the seventh century the Church in the East came under the attack of Islamic armies. The eighth century saw the continuing conversion of European peoples. In 800 Charlemagne was crowned as Holy Roman Emperor. He promoted Christianity, but he also renewed church-state ties, laying the groundwork for corruption and decay in the Church during the ninth and tenth centuries, a period sometimes designated as the Dark Ages.

The eleventh and twelfth centuries saw such diverse movements as the Crusades to free the Holy Land, monastic reform, establishment of the great universities, and Gothic architecture. A serious setback occurred in 1054 when divisions between the East and West led to the schism or separation of the Eastern Church from Rome. The thirteenth century was marked by the presence of great saints like Francis, Dominic, and Thomas Aquinas. Unfortunately, the fourteenth century brought confusion to the Church when the popes moved from Rome to Avignon in France from 1305 to 1376 and when two or three men claimed to be pope from 1378 to 1417. In the fifteenth century corruption among many Church leaders and increasing interference by the secular authorities in ecclesiastical matters made reform imperative. There were many saintly Catholics, both clergy and laity, who called for renewal, but their messages were not heeded.

In 1517 Martin Luther, a Catholic monk, posted his "Ninety-five Theses" on a chapel door in Wittenburg, Germany, calling for an end to the abuses in the Church. He wanted reform, not a new church; but poor communications, stubbornness on the part of Luther and his Catholic counterparts, and interference by secular authorities led him to a "protestant" position, accepting the Bible as the only true authority and teaching salvation by faith alone. He was followed in his break from the Church by Jean Calvin (Switzerland), John Knox (Scotland), Henry VIII (England), and many others. Division followed division, and Christianity has since been split into thousands of churches.

The Protestant break from the Catholic Church finally shocked Catholic leadership into serious efforts for reform. The Council of Trent (1545-1563) clarified Catholic belief, corrected abuses, and set up the seminary system for the education of clergy. New religious orders like the Jesuits arose to aid in renewal. Many great saints promoted spiritual growth in Europe and led missionary activities in the New World and elsewhere, bringing hundreds of thousands of new members into the Church. The Church suffered more persecutions, like those of the French Revolution, for example, but survived them.

Since the Council of Trent there has been a steady movement in the leadership of the Catholic Church away from secular entanglements toward a more spiritual focus. New understandings of church-state separation arose from the Constitution of the United States. Scientific knowledge advanced from the seventeenth century to the twentieth century, and the Church has had to reexamine the relationship of faith and science. The coming of so many

Catholic immigrants to North and South America and the growth of the Church in the Americas has had an important impact on the Church. The success of missionary activities all over the world have helped to make the Church more universal.

At the end of the twentieth century, there are about nine hundred million Catholics, almost one sixth of the world's population. The last one hundred years have seen a succession of remarkable popes who have led the Church through rapidly changing times to a point where the papacy is perhaps more respected and more influential than it has ever been. But these popes have also pointed out the ongoing need for reform if the Church is to be faithful to Christ. The Second Vatican Council, a gathering in Rome of all the Catholic bishops of the world in the 1960s, restated Catholic beliefs for the modern world and instituted many changes in worship and structure, encouraging Catholics to renew their efforts to follow Christ. There are many challenges facing the Church today: materialism, atheism, immorality, the unstable condition of the international political scene, a shortage of vocations to the priesthood and religious life, just to name a few. And all its members are human, as fallible as were Peter and the apostles. Yet the Church is still the Body of Christ, and we can trust that he will continue to guide and strengthen the Church as he has from the beginning.

## One, Holy, Catholic, and Apostolic Church (C 811–70)

From New Testament times to the present, through all the ups and downs of history, the Church has described itself as "one holy catholic and apostolic." These words were used by the Councils of Nicea and Constantinople in the fourth century, and they are used by Catholics today when we pray the Nicene Creed at Mass. What do they mean?

The Church is *one*. We believe that the Catholic Church is built on the rock of Peter's faith (Matthew 16:18) and that it is united under Peter's successor, the pope. We do not say that other churches have no relationship to Christ. But we believe that Christ wants all his followers to be united in him. He prayed "that they may all be one" (John 17:21). Vatican II taught that while divisions exist, we should see the good in other churches, and work and pray for unity.

The Church is *holy*. "You are…a holy nation" (1 Peter 2:9).

Christ died to make us holy. This does not mean that we are sinless (as is obvious from our history), but that we are given a share in the holiness of God through baptism and are called to reject sin and live in union with Christ (Philippians 1:4-11).

The Church is *catholic*. This word, first used in reference to Christians by Saint Ignatius of Antioch around A.D. 100, means "universal" and refers to Christ's Church throughout the world. When divisions arose among believers, *catholic* also became a proper word, like a first name. Thus Augustine spoke of himself as a "Catholic Christian." We are proud to be Catholic, and we believe in our union with other followers of Christ over all the earth. Together, we are "Christ's body" (1 Corinthians 12:27).

The Church is *apostolic*. This means that the Church traces its authority back to Jesus through the apostles: Jesus commissioned the apostles (Acts 1:8; 9:15), who commissioned others (2 Timothy 1:6) who did the same through the centuries up to the pope and bishops today. The Church is apostolic because it faithfully proclaims the teaching of the apostles and ministers to others as they did. The Church is apostolic in the sense that it is missionary: an apostle is "one who is sent," and the whole Church is sent to preach the gospel to the world. Our Church, then, is "built upon the foundation of the apostles" (Ephesians 2:20).

### The Church: The Sacrament of Christ (C 787–810)

Jesus made God visible on earth, and theologians say that Christ is the "sacrament" of God, meaning that Christ was a visible sign to his contemporaries of the invisible God. The Church makes Christ visible today, and so is the "sacrament" of Christ, a visible sign of his presence in our world.

Christ put a great deal of trust in his apostles and in us! He depends upon us to continue his work, and the success of this mission depends to a great extent on how well we fulfill our role of being Christ to the world. Before Jesus was crucified, he had his own mortal body through which he could speak, listen, touch, forgive, heal, comfort, share, pray, love, unite, and bless. Now we are his Body.

We give Christ our lips to speak his words of love and comfort. We give him our hearing to listen to the troubled. We give him our eyes to look with love upon others. We give him our hands to touch the lonely. When we forgive, Christ forgives and brings peace to those seeking pardon. When we heal, Christ heals; when we comfort the sorrowful, Christ consoles. Christ needs our generosity so that he may help the poor. He needs our prayers so that his prayer can be lifted up to the Father from every age and place. Through our love, Christ's love takes human form. When we work for unity, we answer Christ's prayer for unity, "that they may all be one" (John 17:21). When we bless, Christ blesses.

We are members of the Body of Christ. Paul writes, "So we, though many, are one body in Christ and individually parts of one another. Since we have gifts that differ according to the grace given to us, let us exercise them" (Romans 12:5-6). Parents raising their children, students attending class and participating in school activities, adults at their jobs and professions, priests and religious in their ministries, the elderly in nursing homes...all are the Body of Christ. "Now you are Christ's body, and individually parts of it" (1 Corinthians 12:27).

As we look at the weaknesses in ourselves and in other members of the Church, we may feel that it is presumptuous to see ourselves as the "body of Christ." Yet "Christ loved the church and handed himself over for her to sanctify her, cleansing her by the bath of water with the word, that he might present to himself the church in splendor, without spot or wrinkle or any such thing, that she might be holy and without blemish" (Ephesians 5:25-27). The "church in splendor" will exist only in the fullness of eternity, but the Church on earth, which needed cleansing in New Testament times and needs cleansing today, is nourished and cherished by Christ "because we are members of his body" (Ephesians 5:30).

We are nourished also by our communion with the "church in splendor," with the saints in heaven. In our next chapter, we will examine our Catholic understanding of the "communion of saints."

### *Questions for Discussion or Reflection*

In what ways can the Trinity be a doctrine that has practical implications for your daily life? What human characteristic of Jesus do you like most? Is it possible to really love Christ without loving the human beings who make up the Church? Do you think that Christ needs you? In what sense are you Christ in your home? at work? in your social life? at church?

### *Activities*

Read Romans 8:14-17 and Galatians 4:4-7. Think of God as the Goal of your life and as the One from whom you come—the Father. Think of Jesus at your side, teaching you to call God "Father," standing with you as you pray—the Son. Think of God within you, inspiring you to lift up your heart to the Father, giving depth and feeling to your prayer—the Holy Spirit.

*This prayer of praise to the Trinity is said often by Catholics:*

### *Prayer of Praise*

Glory to the Father, and to the Son, and to the Holy Spirit; as it was in the beginning, is now, and will be for ever. Amen.

# CHAPTER SIX
## Jesus Gives Us
## Communion With the Saints

Walk into anyone's home and you are likely to find pictures of family members from generations past—grandparents who moved to the area, parents who built the house, relatives who form the family tree. If you inquire, you may be shown mementos like the books they read, the jewelry they wore, keepsakes they treasured, and diaries they kept. We like to recall our past, search for roots, and delve into our background in a quest for information about our ancestors.

We who are Catholic remember those who have gone before us in our Church family. We hope to learn from the saints and so come to a deeper knowledge of ourselves. We look to them for inspiration, courage, and hope.

### Remembering and Honoring the Saints (C 957, 1159–62)

Some people criticize Catholics for honoring the saints. But it is biblical to remember and honor them. The eleventh chapter of Hebrews is a "verbal memorial" in honor of the holy men and women of the Old Testament. Hebrews 13:7 advises: "Remember your leaders who spoke the word of God to you. Consider the outcome of their way of life and imitate their faith."

It is also natural to honor great people from the past. In our national capital, the Washington Monument, the Lincoln Memorial, and many other shrines and statues honor government and military leaders. Catholics name churches after saints and erect statues to honor spiritual leaders.

## The Communion of Saints (C 946–62)

We do more than remember. We believe in a union, called the communion of saints, which includes all those who are joined to Christ on earth, in heaven, and in purgatory.

We believe that the saints care about us and watch over us, that they pray for us, and that we can pray with them. We base these beliefs on holy Scripture. In the Book of Revelation, the saints in heaven are pictured as offering to God the prayers of God's people: "Each of the elders held a harp and gold bowls filled with incense, which are the prayers of the holy ones" (5:8). 2 Maccabees 15:12-15 reports a vision in which the martyred high priest Onias and the prophet Jeremiah pray for the Jewish nation; this demonstrates the Jewish belief that saints are aware of earthly events and pray for us. Moses and Elijah appear with Jesus at the Transfiguration and talk with him about his coming Passion and death (Luke 9:28-36). Jesus speaks of the "joy in heaven over one sinner who repents" (Luke 15:7). The Letter to the Hebrews compares life to a race we run while the great heroes of the past are in the stands cheering us on. "Therefore, since we are surrounded by so great a cloud of witnesses, let us… persevere in running the race that lies before us" (Hebrews 12:1).

These passages imply interaction between those in heaven and those on earth, and we should be aware of the presence and loving care of the saints. Those who are "in heaven" are close to the knowledge and love of God and, therefore, are more aware of our needs and more devoted to us than they were on earth. We are never alone, for we live "in communion" with the saints.

## Praying to the Saints (C 956, 2683–84)

Sometimes Catholics are asked, "Why do you pray to the saints? Why don't you just pray directly to God?" We should first note that "pray" is used in two different ways by Catholics. We "pray" to God as the source of all blessings. We "pray" to the saints in the sense that we ask them to pray with us and for us. This is illustrated in two prayers frequently said by Catholics. In the Lord's Prayer, we ask God to "give us this day our daily bread" and to "forgive us our trespasses." In the Hail Mary, we ask Mary to "pray for us sinners."

Catholics are sometimes criticized for "worshiping" the saints, especially Mary. We do not worship the saints. *Worship* and *adoration* are terms that refer to the act of acknowledging God as the Supreme Being. We Catholics worship and adore God alone.

But why pray to the saints at all? The answer lies in the importance of prayer with others and for others. Jesus places a special importance in common prayer: "For where two or three are gathered together in my name, there am I in the midst of them" (Matthew 18:20). Since there is a particular value in praying with others, and since the Bible shows that those in heaven pray for us, it certainly makes sense for us to pray *with* the saints.

It also makes sense for us to ask them to pray *for* us. Paul wrote to the Colossians: "Persevere in prayer, being watchful in it with thanksgiving; at the same time, pray for us, too" (4:2-3). Paul prayed directly to God, but he felt it was important to have others intercede for him. If the prayers of those on earth have value, then how much more so the prayers of the saints who stand at the throne of God in heaven!

The prayers of others are needed, not to convince God to bless us but to open us up to the blessings God wants us to receive. Since that is the case, the more intercessors we have on earth and in heaven, the more we can be freed of the hindrances of sin and unbelief which keep us from receiving God's assistance.

We can and should pray directly to God. But our prayers to God take on new life and power when we consciously join them to the prayers of the saints. And each time we pray with the saints, including friends and family members who have died in Christ, we are reminded that we are never alone. Prayer to the saints "keeps us in touch" with them until we join them in heaven.

## Canonization of Saints (C 828)

The New Testament addressed Christians on earth as the "saints," but Catholic tradition very quickly began to apply the term to holy individuals who had entered eternal life, especially to those who had been martyred for Christ. Details of their sufferings, last words, and death were recalled. The apostles, martyrs, and holy people were remembered by the Church and invoked in prayer. The tombs of the martyrs were regarded as holy places. When the Church spread throughout the world, groups of believers began to honor their own saints. As stories were told about the great people of the past, legends began to spring up, and it was not always possible to distinguish fact from fiction in the lives of the saints.

By the tenth century the Church developed a process called "canonization," in which those who had led holy lives were formally named saints. In the sixteenth century a special commission was set up to study the lives of saintly individuals and to make recommendations to the pope about their canonization. More recently there has been much historical research into the lives of the saints, and the Church has limited its formal recognition to saints whose lives could be studied and verified. The Catholic Church has a liturgical "calendar of the saints," honoring those whose lives have a special importance for the whole Church. Many other saints are remembered only in specific localities or by particular groups.

## Devotions in Honor of the Saints (C 1173, 1195)

The Catholic Church has a holy day of obligation in honor of "All Saints" on the first of November. This feast acknowledges that there are innumerable human beings who have been saved by the blood of Christ, "a great multitude, which no one could count, from every nation, race, people, and tongue" (Revelation 7:9). We all have our "own saints" before the throne of God.

Masses are celebrated in honor of the saints often on weekdays, and occasionally on Sundays. This practice encourages us to remember their lives and to ask them to pray for us. There are prayers and private devotions honoring various saints, and Catholics are encouraged to pray to the saints in their own words.

It goes without saying that devotion to the saints should help us grow in our commitment to Jesus Christ. The saints direct us to Christ and would not want our enthusiasm for them to distract us from Jesus. Real devotion to the saints sees Christ's face mirrored in his faithful followers and leads us closer to him.

## The Saints: Models of Christlike Living
## (C 1717, 2030, 2156)

When families get together, they often talk about relatives who have gone before them. They remember a grandfather who donated land for a church cemetery and the aunt who worked day and night to support her family during the Depression. Such recollections give us a sense of oneness with the past and encourage us to persevere in our efforts to lead worthwhile lives. In a similar way our Catholic family remembers our "relatives" in the faith. They form a family tree that is rooted in Jesus Christ. They teach us how to follow Christ in every way of life, and they encourage us to persevere.

Carpenters can look to Saint Joseph to discover that they can be "just" men using hammer and saw. Young people can see in Saint Maria Goretti a model of purity and devotion to Jesus. Mothers can imitate Saint Elizabeth Ann Seton in her dedication to her family. Farmers can learn from Saint Isidore that there is holiness in working the soil, caring for animals, and sharing food with the poor. There are "patron saints" for every vocation and way of life. By studying the lives of the saints, we discover how sanctity may be found in every place and age.

What is just as important, we find that the saints were human beings like us. They had faults and failings, even the greatest of them. When we deny Christ by sin, we can turn to Peter, for he knew what it was like to fail and to receive forgiveness from the Lord. When we fear that we have squandered too many years in petty foolishness, we can ask for the help of Saint Augustine, who prayed, "Too late have I loved Thee, O Beauty ever Ancient, ever New. Too late have I loved Thee." When we sin, or when we succeed, there are saints who walked the path before us and found their way to heaven. They inspire us and lead us on.

## The Souls in Purgatory (C 958, 1030–32)

Catholics believe that some people may experience death when they are neither cut off from God by serious sin nor perfectly free from all venial sin. They need further "purification" from sin to achieve the holiness necessary to stand in God's presence where "nothing unclean will enter" (Revelation 21:27). The Catholic Church teaches that such individuals can be helped by the prayers of others. This belief goes back to Old Testament times and finds expression in the New Testament as well.

Some Jewish soldiers fighting in the war for independence under Judas Maccabeus had been slain in battle. They were found to be wearing pagan amulets, a practice forbidden by Jewish law. Their comrades prayed for the dead "that the sinful deed might be fully blotted out." Then Judas "took up a collection among all his soldiers, amounting to two thousand silver drachmas, which he sent to Jerusalem to provide for an expiatory sacrifice." The Bible comments that this was "holy and pious" and affirms that "he made atonement for the dead that they might be freed from this sin" (2 Maccabees 12:38-46).

The New Testament (2 Timothy 1:18) contains a prayer for one who had died: Paul says of his friend, Onesiphorus: "May the Lord grant him to find mercy from the Lord on that day." As the footnotes in the *New American Bible* point out, Onesiphorus apparently died before this letter was written. His family is mentioned twice (2 Timothy 1:16; 4:19), though it was Onesiphorus himself who was helpful to Paul in prison and rendered much service to the community at Ephesus. Because Paul complains of abandonment by all in Asia during his second imprisonment and trial, the assistance of Onesiphorus seems to have been given to Paul during his first Roman imprisonment (A.D. 61-63).

Inspired by these passages, believers prayed for their beloved dead from New Testament times, as evidenced by inscriptions in the Roman catacombs, early Christian burial places. In the fourth century Saint Monica made this deathbed request of her son, Saint Augustine: "One thing only I ask you, that you remember me at the altar of the Lord wherever you may be."

The practice of praying for the deceased was unchallenged until a controversy over indulgences at the time of Martin Luther. An indulgence is a declaration that certain prayers or actions of Christians have special value because they share in the grace of Christ and in the good works of the saints. The Church applies indulgences to the deceased, following the biblical teaching of Paul that members of Christ's Body can help one another (1 Corinthians 12:12-27) and that the merits of one member can be applied to others (Colossians 1:24). However, indulgences can be misunderstood and abused. Some abuses existed at the time of Luther. In reacting against them, Luther unfortunately went to the extreme of denying the validity of indulgences. He then rejected the practice of praying for the dead altogether. As a result, many Protestant denominations today do not pray for the deceased.

The Catholic Church has continued to pray for the dead, and this prayer has brought consolation and peace to the bereaved. When we stand at the grave of a loved one, we are not helpless onlookers. By God's grace we can reach across space and time to assist the faithful departed by our prayers. We believe that their prayers can help us as well. Death may cause physical separation, but it cannot destroy the spiritual bonds Christ has forged between us and those who have died in his grace.

## Mary: Our Blessed Mother
## (C 484–511, 721–26, 963–75, 2673–79)

Catholics give special honor to Mary, the Mother of Jesus Christ. She was chosen by God to be the Mother of God's only Son. Without doubt, this was the greatest privilege and the most significant of all human accomplishments, after those of Jesus. The Bible states that "all ages" will call Mary blessed (Luke 1:48) and, in obedience to this passage, generations of Catholics have been proud to call Mary their "Blessed Mother."

Mary has a unique place in Scripture. She is greeted by the angel Gabriel with words that show God's esteem for her: "Hail, favored one! The Lord is with you" (Luke 1:28). She is the faithful "handmaid of the Lord" (Luke 1:38) who assents to God's will. Elizabeth salutes Mary, "Most blessed are you among women" (Luke 1:42). In the Gospel of John, it is Mary who occasions the first miracle worked by Jesus (John 2:1-11), and John's use of the term *woman* in reference to Mary may well be an allusion to the "woman" of Genesis: Mary is the "new Eve" and Mother of all the living. Mary is again addressed as "woman" at the Crucifixion. "When Jesus saw his mother and the disciple there whom he loved, he said to his mother, 'Woman, behold, your son.' Then he said to the disciple, 'Behold, your mother'" (John 19:26-27). The Beloved Disciple may be seen to represent all Christians, and Mary is given to us as our Mother.

The Bible clearly teaches that we are the Body of Christ. Since there is a mystical, but real, identification of Jesus with his followers, the Mother of Jesus is our Mother too. And the very fact that Mary is our Mother should help us realize what Vatican II taught explicitly—that Mary is one of us, a member of the Church, and one of those redeemed by Christ.

## The Immaculate Conception (C 490–94)

The Catholic Church believes that Mary was conceived without sin. Many people confuse this doctrine with that of the virginal conception of Christ, but the two are different. The doctrine of the Immaculate Conception teaches that Mary, by God's grace, was preserved from all stain of original sin and that she herself never sinned. When the doctrine was proclaimed by Pope Pius IX in 1854, he explained that Mary shared in the redemptive act of Christ in that she was saved by the foreseen merits of Christ. The Immaculate Conception is an example of Catholic doctrine that is not clearly taught in Scripture but which, congruent with Scripture, was believed universally by Catholics for centuries before it was formally defined as doctrine by the pope.

### Mother of God (C 495)

Catholics believe that Mary is truly the Mother of God. This does not mean that Mary was the source of the divine nature of Jesus, but that she was the Mother of his human nature and that there was no time when the human Jesus was not God. The second Person of the Trinity existed from all eternity, but when the "Word became flesh," Jesus was both human and divine from the first moment of his conception. Mary was not the Mother of a human being who was adopted as God's Son. She was Mother of Jesus Christ, both God and human. Therefore, it is proper for us to call Mary the "Mother of God."

### Ever-Virgin (C 499–507)

The Bible teaches that Mary was a virgin when she gave birth to Christ. The Catholic Church has always believed that Mary remained a virgin her whole life. Early Christian writers agreed that Jesus had no blood brothers and sisters and that Mary remained a virgin. Saint Jerome (345-420) wrote that "learned men going back to apostolic times" testified to the perpetual virginity of Mary. Early Protestants, like Luther and Calvin, also believed in Mary's perpetual virginity. More recently, however, their belief has been questioned.

The New Testament speaks of "brothers" and "sisters" of Jesus. But it never refers to other children of Mary or Joseph, so it is impossible to prove from the Bible that Jesus actually had blood brothers or sisters. But there are many passages which indicate that he did not. For example, two of those who are called brothers of Jesus, namely James and Joseph (Matthew 13:55), are later identified as sons of a woman other than Mary (Matthew 27:56). If Mary had other children, it is difficult to explain why Jesus, as he hung on the cross, would have given Mary into the care of the Beloved Disciple (John 19:26-27). The word *brothers* is frequently used in the New Testament for the followers of Jesus. (See, for instance, John 20:17-18; Luke 8:21.) So the New Testament does not provide any real evidence against the Church's belief. And early teachers like Jerome had no reason for stating that Jesus was an only child except that he actually was an only child! The Church has been guided by the same Holy Spirit who inspired the Bible, and the Church teaches that the brothers and sisters of Jesus were actually relatives and followers. The Church believes that Mary remained ever a virgin.

What is the importance of this belief? It points to the uniqueness of Jesus as the only Son of God. Mary and Joseph witnessed the miracle of Jesus' conception and birth. They realized that God had entrusted them with the greatest treasure in the history of the world, God's only Son. They understood that their task in life was to nurture and protect the Savior of the human race. Many years later, Jesus would speak of those who renounced marriage "for the sake of the kingdom of heaven" (Matthew 19:12). It cannot be surprising that Mary and Joseph would have wanted to give up their right to have other children in order to dedicate their lives exclusively to the care of God's Son. Mary's perpetual virginity is, therefore, another witness to the divinity of Jesus Christ.

## The Assumption (C 966)

The doctrine of the Assumption is the only clearly infallible statement made by a pope in the last one hundred years. It was defined in 1950 by Pope Pius XII, not on his own initiative but in answer to millions of petitions from all over the world. Like the Immaculate Conception, the Assumption of Mary was accepted by Catholics for centuries before it became dogma. This doctrine proclaims that at the end of Mary's life on earth, Christ gave her victory over death, and her body shared fully in his Resurrection as ours will at the end of time. Because Mary never sinned, she was able to experience complete union with her Son, Jesus. This doctrine is a sign of hope because it points the way to heaven for us, who are, like Mary, members of the Church.

## Apparitions of Mary (C 67)

Mary is our Mother, and Catholics have experienced her intercession in many ways. Generations of believers have praised Mary as one who has led them to the grace of God. Many trustworthy and holy individuals have reported visions of Mary, often accompanied by messages that have been the source of countless blessings. Shrines at the sites of such appearances are visited by millions of people every year, most notably at Our Lady of Guadalupe in Mexico, at Lourdes in France, and at Fatima in Portugal.

The Catholic Church does not require that its members believe in such appearances, but there have been official declarations that some apparitions and the messages associated with them are not contrary to Catholic doctrine and are worthy of belief. We believe on the evidence of Scripture that God sends angels as messengers, and it is reasonable to believe that Jesus can send his Mother as an emissary. Many miracles of healing have occurred at Marian shrines; hundreds of them have been carefully studied by medical bureaus and have been declared to be beyond any medical explanation. The shrine at Lourdes is especially noted for its miracles and the care with which any reported miracles are examined by doctors, non-Catholic as well as Catholic. Anyone who studies these miracles, as they have been described in numerous books and magazine articles, cannot help but be amazed at the evident presence of God's power and grace working through the intercession of Mary.

Jesus said that we can judge a tree by its fruit, and we can see the good fruit of God's blessings flowing from Guadalupe, Lourdes, and Fatima. They are evidence of God's loving care and of Mary's maternal affection for us.

## Devotions in Honor of Mary (C 971)

Mary has been honored in great works of architecture like Notre Dame in Paris, in beautiful music like Schubert's "*Ave Maria*," and in priceless masterpieces like the "Pietà." Churches, religious orders, universities, hospitals, streets, and cities have been named for Mary. But the greatest respect the Catholic Church pays to Mary is through the liturgical feasts in her honor.

Mary has a special place at Christmas, the birthday of Jesus. One week later, New Year's Day is celebrated by Catholics as a holy day under the title of Mary, Mother of God. The Solemnity of Mary's Assumption is observed as a holy day on the fifteenth of August, as is the Solemnity of the Immaculate Conception on the eighth of December. Many other liturgical celebrations bring Mary to mind at various times of the year.

There are nonliturgical prayers honoring Mary that are well known to most Catholics. The Hail Mary is one of the first prayers memorized by Catholic children. The first part is taken from the Bible and the second part asks Mary to "pray for us sinners now and at the hour of our death." The rosary recalls the great mysteries of our salvation, and through it Mary brings us closer to her Son. There are hymns, novenas, and litanies to Mary. Many Catholics wear medals, such as the miraculous medal, to honor Mary and to remind themselves of Mary's loving care. In many parishes May is observed as the month of Mary with processions and May crownings. October is set aside as the month of the holy rosary. In these and many other ways, Catholics show their love to Mary and ask her to help us grow closer to her Son, Jesus.

## What a Family! (C 960–62)

Why honor the saints? Why pray to the saints? Why pray for the souls in purgatory? Because it's natural to remember our loved ones, to ask friends to pray for us, and to pray for our friends. Because it is a grand thing to belong to a good family, and Christ has called us to belong to the great family of believers, present and past, because all of us—believers on earth, saints in heaven, souls in purgatory—are one in the communion of saints. "So then you are no longer strangers and sojourners, but you are fellow citizens with the holy ones and members of the household of God, built upon the foundation of the apostles and prophets, with Christ Jesus himself as the capstone" (Ephesians 2:19-20). Indeed, what a family!

And as members of this family we are destined one day to change our dwelling place from earth to heaven. This happens through death and resurrection, as we shall see in the next chapter.

### Questions for Discussion or Reflection

In your own words answer the questions, "Why do Catholics pray to the saints? Why don't they pray directly to God?" Do you have a favorite saint? Why does that saint appeal to you?

### Activities

At baptism most Catholics are named after a saint. Write a brief description of your patron saint. Try to become more familiar with that saint's life. If you attend a Catholic Church named after a saint, try to discover why that saint was chosen. Look through a Catholic magazine, such as the *Liguorian*. Search for articles on the lives of saints or for other references to saints.

If you would like to learn more about Mary, the Mother of Jesus, you may want to read *Morning Star...Christ's Mother and Ours*, Liguori Publications (see Bibliography).

*A prayer Catholics say often is the Hail Mary:*

Hail Mary, full of grace. The Lord is with thee. Blessed art thou among women, and blessed is the fruit of thy womb, Jesus. Holy Mary, Mother of God, pray for us sinners, now and at the hour of our death. Amen.

# CHAPTER SEVEN
## Jesus Brings Us
## to Fullness of Life

S unlight streamed through her window, and Annie wheeled her chair into its warmth. Bright yellow daffodils bouncing in the wind outside made her remember an Easter dream sixty years before. She had only two weeks to wait until the birth of her first child. She was sitting at a window admiring the flowers near her porch steps when she must have fallen asleep. She began to dream, and in her dream she spoke with the child in her womb…

Hello, Johnny. *What? Who are you?* I'm your mother. *Mother? What's a mother?* Johnny, I'm the one, along with your father, who brought you into this world. *Oh? Then where are you? Why can't I see you?* You can't see me because you're living inside me. But soon you'll be born, and then we'll see each other. *Born? What does that mean?* Well, Johnny, you've been growing, and there's not enough room for you there. The life-support system that's keeping you alive won't work much longer. *You mean I'm going to die?* No, you won't die, you'll just begin to live in a new way. *Why should I believe that? I can't see you. Maybe you're not even there. Maybe I'm all alone and just imagining this.* Johnny, you don't think you just came from nothing, do you? Where you're living is real, but the world is much bigger than you think. When you're out here you'll grow tall and strong; you'll run and play; you'll make friends; you'll go hiking in the woods; you'll have a puppy. You'll… *Wait a minute. What are friends? What are woods? What's a puppy?* Friends and woods and puppies are…Johnny, I can't explain them because there's nothing like them where you are. The more I try to explain, the more impossible they'll seem to you. You'll just have to wait and see. *Now I know I'm imagining this. I'm going to die, and I'm afraid.* Johnny, don't be afraid. I know this sounds hard to believe, and I can't really explain it to you, but it's real. Maybe this will help: do you know what your feet are? *Yes, and I have ten toes too!* That's right, Johnny. But what good are they to you in there? What can you use them for? *Nothing.* Right, Johnny, but you have them because there is an earth here for you to walk and run on. Your feet wouldn't make any sense if there weren't a world out here. Can you believe that? *I'd like to, really I would. But I'm afraid.* I know, and what you're afraid of, your birth, will have to come. There will be some pain and darkness. But then there will be light and life, more life than you can imagine. All I can say is that I've been through what you'll go through, and I'll be waiting here for you with open arms and a big smile. What you think of as death you'll find is really birth!

"That dream seemed so real," Annie thought. Two weeks later her son was born. He had grown into a man she'd always been proud of. He'd soon be coming at Easter to visit her at the nursing home….

*Annie.* A voice startled her out of her thoughts. An aide perhaps? She turned, but saw no one. Just the crucifix on the wall above her dresser. *Annie.* She heard the voice again, but this time it seemed to come from within. She understood. She closed her eyes and prayed, "Yes, Lord?"

*Annie, it's almost time for you to come home.* You mean I'm going to die? *No, Annie, you'll soon be born. You'll soon begin to live in a new way.* Lord, I'm afraid. Sometimes I doubt and wonder if you are really there. I wish I could see you face to face. *That's not possible now, Annie, because I'm on the other side of death. But you don't think you came from nowhere, do you?* No, but sometimes heaven seems like a fairy tale. *Well, I can't describe heaven any more than you could explain your world to Johnny before he was born.* I suppose so, Lord, but I'm still afraid. *I know, Annie, but think of your heart. Has it ever really been satisfied? Have you ever been completely happy?* No, because *your heart is made for God and for eternity. Johnny's feet were made for walking on earth, and your heart was made for heaven.* I'm still afraid, Lord. *Yes, Annie, and what you fear will have to come. There will be some pain and darkness. But then there will be light and life, more life than you can imagine. All I can say is that I've been through what you'll go through, and I'll be waiting here for you with open arms and a big smile. And what you think of as death you'll find is really birth!*

"Amen, Lord," Annie whispered. And she knew that her dream was real.

## Death as Birth (C 988–1019)

We who are Catholic believe that death is not just an end but a new beginning. Perhaps the best way to understand this is to compare death with birth. We spent nine months in the womb of our mother. Then we outgrew our environment, and our life-support system could no longer sustain us. We "died" to life in the womb as everything keeping us alive seemed to fall apart. But "death" turned out to be birth, and we found ourselves suddenly in the light, living in a new way we could never have imagined. We found ourselves breathing and eating, using a new life-support system we could not have dreamed of in the womb. We found ourselves in a new world where there were opportunities for growth, knowledge, and love which far surpassed anything in the womb.

Death is really a second birth. Our life-support system, our body, will wear out because of age, illness, or accident. Everything that keeps us alive will seem to fall apart. But death will turn out to be birth once again, as darkness turns into day and we find ourselves suddenly in the Light, fully alive at last, face to face with Jesus Christ, in a new world with opportunities for growth, knowledge, and love which far surpass anything on earth.

How will this happen? We can't say for sure, although people who have had near-death experiences seem to have at least peeked into the doorway of the life to come. They tell of light, of peace, of being in touch with loved ones in ways unimaginable, of knowing they are loved, of being sure that God is, of having what they describe as a "spiritual body."

Paul wrote: "What you sow is not brought to life unless it dies. And what you sow is not the body that is to be but a bare kernel of wheat, perhaps, or of some other kind....So also is the resurrection of the dead. It is sown corruptible; it is raised incorruptible. It is sown dishonorable; it is raised glorious. It is sown weak; it is raised powerful. It is sown a natural body; it is raised a spiritual body" (1 Corinthians 15:36-37,42-44).

Because Christ died and rose, death will be birth. Because Christ rose, Paul assures us, we too shall be "brought to life" (1 Corinthians 15:22). Our resurrection and the eternal life that will follow are essential doctrines of our faith. Trusting in Jesus, we can even look forward to the moment when we shall be born and say, not just with resignation but with joy and hope: "Father, into your hands I commend my spirit" (Luke 23:46).

## The Particular Judgment (C 1020–22)

The Bible tells us that "it is appointed that human beings die once, and after this the judgment" (Hebrews 9:27). At the moment of our death, we will stand in the presence of God, seeing our years on earth as God sees them. We will understand the evil of sin with complete clarity, and we will grasp the full extent of Christ's love for us. If our fundamental direction in life has been toward God and if we have died in God's grace, we will be attracted to God's love in an ecstasy of gratitude and peace. If our fundamental direction has been away from God, so that we have died in unrepented mortal sin, we will be repulsed by the very love which called us into existence. This is the particular judgment: to stand in God's presence as we really are, to be judged by our own conscience, to be judged by the God of holiness and justice and love.

Many people who have been through a near-death experience report that soon after they leave their physical body they see an "instantaneous playback" of the events of their lives. Time seems to be suspended, for even if it takes only a few moments for doctors to revive them, they have enough "time" to review their whole life. Many say that they return to this life with an appreciation of the importance of love and knowledge and with new insight into the value of other things. Whether this experience is the beginning of the particular judgment is uncertain, but it can help us understand how the judgment might take place.

Catholics believe that through the particular judgment we become aware of our eternal destiny. In referring to the world to come, Jesus speaks of those who will enter into "eternal life" and of those who will go off to "eternal punishment" (Matthew 25:46). Catholics call eternal life "heaven" and eternal punishment "hell" and believe that those who are free from sin will enter heaven after judgment, but that those who have rejected God through unrepented mortal sin will enter hell. Those individuals who are not guilty of unrepented grave sin but come into God's presence with attachments to venial sins will need to be purified before they enter heaven, and their state of purification is called "purgatory." The reality of judgment, heaven, hell, and purgatory is taught as official doctrine by the Catholic Church.

### Heaven (C 1023–29)

Heaven is referred to in Old Testament books like Wisdom, which mentions the "innocent souls' reward" (2:22), but not all Jews of Jesus' time believed in life after death. The Pharisees professed belief in eternal life; the Sadducees did not.

Jesus left no doubt about the reality of eternal life: "For this is the will of my Father, that everyone who sees the Son and believes in him may have eternal life" (John 6:40). This was no vague promise of reincarnation. Jesus said to the criminal who was crucified with him, "Today you will be with me in Paradise" (Luke 23:43). Just as the person who dies to life in the womb is the one born into this world, so the person who dies to this life is the one who enters eternal life.

We don't know exactly what heaven will be like. Paul says that he was "caught up into Paradise and heard ineffable things, which no one may utter" (2 Corinthians 12:4). John writes, "Beloved, we are God's children now; what we shall be has not yet been revealed. We do know that when it is revealed, we shall be like him, for we shall see him as he is" (1 John 3:2). As our life on earth surpasses life in the womb, so life in heaven will surpass this life. Certainly all that is good, beautiful, interesting, and exciting in this life will be more so in heaven, and what causes grief will pass away: "Then I saw a new heaven and a new earth....God himself will always be with them [as their God]. He will wipe every tear from their eyes, and there shall be no more death or mourning, wailing or pain, [for] the old order has passed away" (Revelation 21:1-4).

The greatest joy of heaven will be to see God "face to face." "Blessed are the clean of heart," promises Jesus, "for they will see God" (Matthew 5:8). Catholic tradition calls this vision of God the "beatific vision" because of the happiness it will bring us. And what an incredible experience it will be to stand in the presence of our Creator, to realize that what we have been longing for since the first moment of our existence is now ours forever, to feel completely loved and to love without limits. If we visualize great moments of joy in this life—time spent with a best friend, holidays with our family, arriving home after a long absence, presentation of a diploma, a safe landing after a perilous flight, word from the doctor that we are cured—and if we put all these moments together, we can begin to imagine the happiness that will be ours when we arrive at our true home in heaven and stand in the presence of God!

Sometimes heaven is pictured as "up there" in the clouds, with saints and angels floating around strumming on harps. But heaven is the state of being joined to God and those who love God. Heaven is where God is, everywhere. It may be that God has created our vast universe because God wants us to have eternity to enjoy it. We will not be limited by space or time, and what an exciting prospect it is to have forever to explore all of creation in the company of our friends, the saints, and angels, and to visit with these great ones forever!

### Purgatory (C 1030–32)

Catholics also believe in a temporary state of purification after death called "purgatory." The Church bases its belief on the biblical teaching of prayer for the dead (2 Maccabees 12:38-46; 2 Timothy 1:18, cited in Chapter Six). If heaven and hell were the only possibilities after death, there would be no reason to pray for the dead. Those in heaven would not need prayers, and those in hell would be beyond the reach of prayer. As a result the Church reasoned to the existence of purgatory, an intermediate state where people can be helped by prayer.

Other Bible passages also point to the existence of purgatory. Jesus says that blasphemy against the Holy Spirit will not be forgiven in this age or in the age to come (Matthew 12:31-32). From this the Church has concluded that some sins can be forgiven in the age to come, in the state we know as purgatory.

Paul's words in 1 Corinthians 3:13-15 have been interpreted as referring to purgatory: "The work of each will come to light, for the Day will disclose it. It will be revealed with fire, and the fire [itself] will test the quality of each one's work. If the work stands that someone built upon the foundation, that person will receive a wage. But if someone's work is burned up, that one will suffer loss; the person will be saved, but only as through fire." At the very least, Paul's words seem to express a belief on his part that purification from sin is possible even beyond the grave, on the "Day" of judgment.

The Catholic Church teaches that there is a state of purification after death. It does not teach that purgatory is a place in the sense that the Moon is a place. Those who are in purgatory are spirits, and they cannot be "located" as we can when we are in our mortal bodies.

Nor does the Church teach that there is physical fire in purgatory. The symbolism of fire has been used to express the real pain of purgatory, but the fire cannot be physical because those in purgatory do not have material bodies that can be burned. The "fire" of purgatory is the fire of God's love: "For our God is a consuming fire" (Hebrews 12:29). Just as fire burns away impurities when gold is refined, so God's love will "burn away" the imperfections that could keep us from being perfectly open to the presence, love, and joy of God.

Popular explanations of purgatory in the past have sometimes included graphic descriptions of the suffering of the "poor souls." However, those in purgatory are assured of heaven and are even closer to the love of God than we are on earth, and as a result they must experience profound joy. At the same time they have a clear realization of the evil of even the smallest sin, and they suffer the pain of knowing that they are not yet ready to enter the joys of heaven.

An illustration may be useful: Sarah and Jim plan to celebrate their first wedding anniversary. Sarah's anniversary gift to Jim will be to cook his favorite meal. Jim promises to be home from work by six-thirty that evening. Sarah prepares the meal with loving care and decorates the table with flowers, candles, and their best linen. But just as Jim leaves his office building, he is greeted by a high school buddy he hasn't seen in years. They start talking about old times, so excited that neither notices the passing of the hours, until Jim glances at his watch. It's seven-fifteen, and now he remembers Sarah and the dinner. As Jim hurries home, he knows that Sarah will understand; she has always been patient and forgiving. But he feels terrible because he realizes that he has let her down. He wants to tell her he is sorry, even though it will be painful to acknowledge his fault and forgetfulness. Sarah will do nothing to cause Jim's suffering. But there is pain in his standing before Sarah, in apologizing, and in receiving her love and forgiveness. It is a pain Jim wants to experience because he knows it will remove any barriers his thoughtlessness might have placed between them.

Purgatory might be like that. When we die we may find ourselves in a situation similar to Jim's. We will realize that we have been less responsive to God's great love than we should have been. We will want to go through the pain of standing in God's presence, acknowledging our failings, and expressing our sorrow so that all barriers we have placed between God's love and ourselves may be removed. It will be a painful process, but one we will gladly endure.

We do not know who might need purgatory, and since those in purgatory are beyond earth's space and time, it is not possible to know "how long" anyone might be there. We pray for those in purgatory because the Bible teaches that they can be helped by our prayers. We know that God is not limited by time, and God can take our prayers of a lifetime and apply them to the needs of a loved one at death. We may pray, then, as long as we wish for our beloved dead.

In teaching the doctrine of purgatory, the Catholic Church shows that God's mercy extends even beyond death. Some individuals, by reason of their cooperation with God's grace, may be ready for heaven at the moment of death. But many of us may die with some imperfections that will keep us from being "comfortable" in God's presence where "nothing unclean will enter" (Revelation 21:27). Purgatory means hope for us, a way we can walk to enter heaven in the life of the world to come.

## Hell (C 1033–37)

Hell is not a pleasant subject, but the New Testament teaches that we can choose to be eternally separated from God, using imagery like fire, wailing, and gnashing of teeth to describe the pain of hell. How literally this imagery is to be taken is uncertain, but it is surely meant to alert us that the suffering of hell will be terrible. Jesus warned us of the chilling words which will be spoken to the condemned: "Depart from me, you accursed, into the eternal fire prepared for the devil and his angels. For I was hungry and you gave me no food, I was thirsty and you gave me no drink" (Matthew 25:41-42).

Sometimes people ask, "If God is merciful, how could God condemn someone to hell forever?" The answer is that God simply ratifies the decision of those who have rejected God by mortal sin. It is true to say that God does not create hell. People do, for hell is essentially the state of separation from God, and people cut themselves off from the love of God when they choose the hatred that is sin. God never forces us, and if we choose to reject God, God will respect our choice.

Imagine this situation: Don and Susan fall in love and are married. Life is full of romance when they are near each other. Don hears music in the sound of Susan's voice. But as a few years go by, the excitement of romance begins to dim for Don. He starts to flirt at the office, and his love for Susan begins to cool. She notices and asks what's wrong, but he evades the question. Susan loves Don as much as ever and would do anything for him, but he cotinues to pull away. Eventually, he has an affair and reaches a point where he cannot stand to be near Susan. Her beauty now repulses him. The sound of her voice grates on his ears. Even though friends tell him that he is a fool, he leaves Susan for another woman.

Now suppose that the other woman and all else that entertains Don are taken away. He is alone in the universe with Susan. Where would he be? In hell, of course. The very person who once brought him such joy and ecstasy now brings him disgust and pain. And why? Not because Susan wants this, for she still loves him, but because he has made decisions that turn her love into something that repulses his whole being.

Hell may be something like that. God loves us, and when we accept and return God's love, we find happiness and joy. But if we turn to evil, God's presence and love seem unreal, even disgusting. As long as we are on this earth and have "playthings" to distract us, we can at least have "fun," if not happiness. When we die, however, and all our toys are taken way, we stand empty-handed before God. But God and God's love are now repugnant to us because of the decisions we have made. The universe is full of God's presence, and the only way we can escape is to fall headlong into the hell of our own selfishness and find company with all those who have made the same awful choice. And why? Not because God wants this, for God still loves us. But because we have made decisions that turn God's love into something that repulses our whole being.

Hell is a dreadful fate. It is eternal misery. And the worst part of hell is that for all eternity the damned will know that the one thing which could bring them happiness, God's love, is what they have set themselves against forever.

## The Second Coming of Christ
## and the General Judgment (C 668–82, 1038–65)

We who are Catholic believe in life after death and in judgment. Christ will come to us when we die. We will see him face to face and be judged at that moment. But the full meaning of our lives will not be complete until the world ends. For example, we may bring someone into the Church; that person, in turn, may help others, resulting in much good down through the ages. An evil life, on the other hand, can have repercussions that last through many centuries. So, at the end of time, Jesus will bring human history to a close in a final judgment, which will not change the results of the particular judgment, but will bring the consequences of our deeds to light.

The Bible and the Church have given such names to the end of the world as the End Time, Parousia, General Judgment, Last Judgment, Day of the Lord, and Second Coming of Christ. In describing these events, the Bible speaks vividly of angels, trumpets, fire, falling stars, and people being caught up in the air (Matthew 24:29-31; 25:31- 46, Mark 13:24-27, 1 Thessalonians 4:16-17; Revelation 20:11-15). These terms are poetic and apocalyptic, and should not be taken as literal descriptions of how the world will end.

In the past few centuries many fanciful theories about the "rapture" and the "thousand-year reign" have been concocted. The "rapture" (taken from 1 Thessalonians 4:16-17) actually refers to the same events as the Second Coming of Christ and the General Judgment. The "thousand-year reign" (taken from Revelation 20:4) simply represents the time between Christ's Resurrection and the end of the world.

The Church has not made a dogmatic statement on the exact meaning of passages describing the end of the world and the final judgment. Science tells us that in time our sun will expand into a "red giant" and consume the planets before it dies out. But scientists are unsure about the ultimate fate of the universe as a whole. We simply do not know how the world will end. We leave this in God's hands and trust that God, with divine wisdom and power, will transform the universe into a "new heaven and a new earth."

Nor does the Church define exactly what is meant by the expression that Jesus will gather his elect at the end of time (Matthew 24:31). Artists paint pictures of bodies rising from graves in response to angelic trumpets, but the resurrection of the body on the last day does not mean the reassembly of the atoms which formed our mortal body on this earth. The essential meaning of the resurrection of the body may be that our risen bodies will have a new relationship to the universe, once time on earth is through. Even now, all things on earth are moving toward their completion. After the last day, when time has ended and all human beings have entered eternity, God's masterpiece will be seen in all its glory, and the elect will be active participants in it.

The Bible teaches that the end of the world will be preceded by signs such as the gospel being preached to all nations (Matthew 24:14) and the conversion of the Jews (Romans 11:25-32). Other signs spoken of in Mark 13, Matthew 24, Luke 21, and elsewhere include wars, confusion, suffering, wickedness, and the rise of an antichrist. These signs are general, and there is little official Catholic teaching about how to understand them because the Church wants us to focus on the main truth that this world is passing away.

Jesus said that even he (as a human being) did not know the day or hour when the world would end (Mark 13:32). In spite of this, various groups down through the centuries have tried to predict the time of the end of the world. They've all, obviously, been wrong!

So we should avoid useless speculation and worry about the end of the world. The world ends for each one of us when we die. What is important is that we always be prepared to meet Jesus. Trusting in God's love and in the salvation won for us by Christ, we even dare to pray with the early believers: *"Marana tha!"* "Come, Lord Jesus!"

### *Questions for Discussion or Reflection*

Have you ever thought of death as birth? as an exciting possibility? What are some great moments of earthly joy that foreshadow the beatific vision? Name some things you want to experience in heaven? What will purgatory be like? Could God do away with hell and still leave us free?

### *Activities*

Picture yourself as Annie (as in the story opening this chapter) and talk with Jesus about death. Imagine yourself trying to explain this life to an unborn child and reflect on the difficulties you would encounter in doing so.

# PART II
# WORSHIP

# CHAPTER EIGHT
## Christ in His Sacraments—
## Baptism and Confirmation

Human life is enriched by celebration and ritual. Balloons and flowers send congratulations at the birth of a child and mark the addition of a new member to the family. Initiation ceremonies commit individuals to particular organizations. Meals give strength and bring families and friends together. Words of forgiveness and a handshake or a hug melt the coldness of a quarrel with the warmth of reconciliation. Ceremony and music and dancing tell the world that a man and woman have joined in marriage. Those who lead—teachers or police or government officials—are commissioned for their tasks. Funny cards and visits encourage a friend in the hospital, and floral wreaths or words of sympathy comfort bereaved family members at the loss of a loved one.

Jesus Christ was no stranger to celebration and ritual. Angels sang at his birth, and he was circumcised according to Jewish law. At the age when Jewish boys become bar mitzvah (a son of the law), he went to the Jerusalem Temple with Mary and Joseph. Jesus shared meals with friends, forgave sinners with words of comfort and peace, changed water into wine to keep the party going at the wedding feast of Cana, commissioned his apostles to teach all nations, healed the sick, and wept at the grave of his friend Lazarus.

The first Christians saw Jesus' presence in all that celebrates the goodness of human life. They knew that Christ had come to sanctify everything we do, that he had entered life as sunlight enters crystal, filling it with light and beauty.

## The Sacraments (C 1076–158, 1187–1209)

How did Christ enter the lives of his followers? The apostles believed that it was through signs of celebration and ritual given them by the Lord. On the first Pentecost, Peter told the crowds, "Repent and be baptized" (Acts 2:38). Paul reminded the Corinthians at the Last Supper that they proclaimed Christ's death and shared his body and blood by doing what he did at the Supper (1 Corinthians 11:23-27). Christ gave new life through the sign of baptism; he was present through the sign of the Eucharist.

At first there was no organized theology of such signs, but one was gradually developed under the guidance of the Holy Spirit. By the thirteenth century the Church recognized seven signs, or sacraments, that had been given us by Christ. The Council of Trent declared as dogma that these are baptism, confirmation, Eucharist, penance, matrimony, holy orders, and anointing of the sick.

These sacraments are "meetings with Christ," where he does today what he did in Palestine two thousand years ago. He gives eternal life through baptism as he offered it to his contemporaries (John 17:2). He pours out the Holy Spirit in confirmation to commit and consecrate us to the Church as he sent the Spirit upon the apostles (Acts 2). He gives us himself in the Eucharist as he gave the apostles his body and blood at the Last Supper (Matthew 26:26-28). He forgives us through penance as he forgave the sinful woman who wept at his feet (Luke 7:36-50). Through matrimony he brings God's grace to husband and wife as he did at the wedding feast of Cana (John 2:1-11). He sends others to teach, lead, and sanctify in holy orders as he sent the apostles (Matthew 28:18-20). Through anointing, he heals as he cured the sick who came to him, or he leads the dying to eternal life as he promised heaven to the thief on the cross (Mark 1:32-34; Luke 23:43).

A sacrament may be defined as a sign from Christ by which he comes to us and gives us his life and love. The sign may be clearly expressed in the Bible, like the water of baptism and the bread and wine of the Eucharist. Or it may be the result of the Church's experience and reflection, such as the exchange of vows in matrimony. Each sacrament includes the use of Scripture. In every sacrament Christ acts through the signs and speaks through Scripture.

Because Christ is truly present through the sacraments, they can always have an effect in our lives. However, we must approach the sacraments with faith and devotion. We need the eyes of faith to look beyond the signs to the reality they contain, and devoted hearts to focus on Christ's presence. Like the two disciples on the way to Emmaus who recognized the risen Jesus as he broke bread with them and opened the Scriptures to them (Luke 24:13-35), we must recognize in the sacraments the risen Jesus giving us new life.

The *Catechism of the Catholic Church* divides the sacraments into three groups: the sacraments of initiation—baptism, confirmation, and Eucharist; the sacraments of healing—penance and anointing of the sick; the sacraments at the service of communion and the mission of the faithful—holy orders and matrimony. We will study them in the order followed in these divisions.

### Baptism—the First Sacrament (C 1210–12)

"It was like a miracle," parents often say of the birth of their child. "God seemed to be there in the hospital room with us!" There are few events more moving than the birth of a child. As the parents hold new life in their arms, they may be filled with faith in God, with hope for their child, and with love for each other as their eyes fill with tears of joy and awe.

But birth can also make us realize how fragile life is and how quickly it passes. Grandparents whisper to new parents, "It seems only yesterday that we were holding you." Life goes swiftly by, and faith can be lost, hopes dashed, and love weakened. If only there were a birth that did not have to end in death! If only we could be "reborn" to a life where faith, hope, and love could not be destroyed!

Jesus came to give us such a birth. By God's grace any human being can be reborn to a new life that will never end. That birth is baptism, the sacrament which unites us to the life of Christ himself and opens for us the pathway to the other sacraments and to eternal life.

### The Origins of Baptism (C 1213–28)

The first mention of baptism in the New Testament is made in reference to John the Baptizer, who invited people to be "baptized" in the Jordan River as a sign of repentance (Matthew 3:1-17).

John's baptism symbolized a desire to be freed of sin and to live more worthily. Jesus was baptized by John, not because he needed to repent but because he wanted to show his oneness with humanity.

John's baptism was not the baptism given by Jesus. John said he was baptizing with water for repentance, but Jesus would baptize with the Holy Spirit (Matthew 3:11). The baptism of Jesus is not merely a symbol of repentance but a powerful action of Jesus that brings God's life to us. As Jesus explained, "No one can enter the kingdom of God without being born of water and Spirit. What is born of flesh is flesh and what is born of spirit is spirit" (John 3:5-6).

After his Resurrection, Jesus told the apostles to "make disciples of all nations, baptizing them in the name of the Father, and of the Son, and of the holy Spirit" (Matthew 28:19). So Peter told his hearers on the first Pentecost, "Repent and be baptized, every one of you, in the name of Jesus Christ for the forgiveness of your sins; and you will receive the gift of the holy Spirit....Those who accepted his message were baptized" (Acts 2:38, 41).

### The Effects of Baptism (C 1262–84)

What does baptism do for us? First, it brings *forgiveness of sins*. Paul wrote: "We were indeed buried with him [Christ] through baptism into death..." (Romans 6:4). This means that we have died to the old life of sin: baptism brings "death" to sin. In traditional Catholic theology, this includes deliverance from original sin (see page 20) and from any personal sins one has committed.

Second, baptism brings *new life*. Paul noted that we have been buried with Christ "so that, just as Christ was raised from the dead by the glory of the Father, we too might live in newness of life" (Romans 6:4). This is the *life of Christ*, traditionally called "sanctifying grace." It is God's love, which gives our actions a special worth in God's sight and offers a pledge of eternal life. Sanctifying grace opens us up to God's assistance, traditionally called "actual grace," helping us to overcome temptation and to imitate Christ in thought, word, and action. We might compare sanctifying grace to the love parents have for their children: a love that is literally life-giving. We can compare actual graces to the many things parents do for their children: acts of protecting, nourishing, teaching, forgiving, and guiding that help children grow and mature.

Third, baptism gives us *union with God*. God wants to be close to us, and joins us to the love of Father, Son, and Holy Spirit through baptism. Scripture refers to this in many ways. A Christian is a "temple of God" in whom "the Spirit of God dwells" (1 Corinthians 3:16). Jesus promised to send the Holy Spirit to be with us always (John 14:15) and promised also, "Whoever loves me will keep my word, and my Father will love him, and we will come to him and make our dwelling with him" (John 14:23). The Church teaches that in baptism we are given the virtues of faith, hope, and love, by which our union with God is nourished and strengthened.

Fourth, baptism confers *membership in the Church*, the Body of Christ. Paul wrote: "For in one Spirit we were all baptized into one body" (1 Corinthians 12:13). That "one body" is the Body of Christ on earth, the Church.

And so there is a life which does not have to end in death. There is "rebirth" to a life where faith, hope, and love cannot be destroyed, because they are given to us by God.

### Baptism and the Church (C 1229–45, 1256)

In New Testament times people who heard the Good News of Christ were baptized soon after professing faith in Jesus (see Acts 2; 8; 10; 16). But when persecutions started, the Church began to require a period of instruction lasting one or more years. The weeks before Easter were a special time of preparation and prayer, leading up to the Easter Vigil celebration when new converts were baptized, confirmed with the Holy Spirit, and given the Eucharist.

At first, baptism was conferred by immersing the candidate. Paul implies this when he says that we are buried with Christ in baptism and rise to new life. In time baptism was also administered by the pouring of water over a candidate's head, perhaps because immersion proved to be inconvenient in colder climates.

Preparation for baptism was shortened when mass conversions began and entire tribes were received into the Church with their leaders. As Christianity spread, the practice of infant baptism became common. It may be that children had been baptized even in New Testament times because families were baptized together, and this presumably included children (Acts 10; 11:14-15; 16:15,33). Baptism of infants would not have seemed strange to

Jewish Christians, for Jews practiced circumcision of boys eight days old (Luke 2:21). After infant baptism became the norm, adults who wished to join the Church were usually instructed by a priest and baptized privately.

In the Catholic Church today baptism may be done by immersion or by pouring water over the head of the candidate. A bishop, priest, or deacon is the usual minister of baptism. In case of necessity, anyone can baptize by intending to do what the Church does and by pouring water over the person's head while saying, "I baptize you in the name of the Father, and of the Son, and of the Holy Spirit."

The water and prayer are the signs essential for a valid baptism, but in the full ceremony of baptism other signs are used. Blessed oil and chrism (oil mixed with balsam) signify the comfort and strength given by the Holy Spirit. A baptismal candle is a reminder that Christ is the light of the world (John 8:12). A white baptismal garment recalls Paul's words: "For all of you who were baptized into Christ have clothed yourselves with Christ" (Galatians 3:27). Sponsors represent the Christian community and help welcome the candidate into the Church.

### Infant Baptism Today (C 1250–55, 1261)

Infant baptism has a long tradition in the Catholic Church going back to its antecedents in Judaism and at least hinted at in the New Testament. It is based on our belief that Christ wants to "take into his arms" the little children of today, just as he embraced the children of his time (Mark 10:13-16). It also shows that we don't have to do anything to earn God's love, which is freely bestowed even upon infants who are cherished by God simply because they are God's children.

However, parents who have their children baptized should have a serious intention of bringing the children up in the faith. In the baptism ceremony Catholic parents make solemn promises to do just that. Parents should pray for and with their children, be the first teachers of the faith to their children by word and example, and lead them to the other sacraments of the Church. If parents have their children baptized and then do not raise them as Catholics, they are denying the children the very life begun by baptism. This is like giving a child physical life and then denying that child food, clothing, and shelter. Parents who do follow baptism with prayer, instruction, and good example give their children the assurance that they are loved and cared for by Jesus.

Some Catholics have been taught that unbaptized infants go to "limbo," a place of eternal natural happiness, without the intimate closeness to God enjoyed by those in heaven. Limbo as the abode of unbaptized infants, however, is not Catholic doctrine. It is a theological opinion not commonly accepted today. The *Catechism of the Catholic Church* notes that the burial Mass for unbaptized infants entrusts them to God's care. It states that God's great mercy and Jesus' tenderness toward children allow us to hope that there is a way of salvation for children who have died without baptism (C 1262). We may trust that Jesus who said, "It is not the will of your heavenly Father that one of these little ones be lost" (Matthew 18:14), welcomes each "little one" with the same warm embrace he gave the children of his time.

## Adult Baptism Today (C 1232-33, 1246–49, 1312)

The Second Vatican Council recommended that the Church renew its way of receiving adult candidates. A revised rite called the Rite of Christian Initiation of Adults (RCIA) was approved by Pope Paul VI in 1972 and has become the norm for the Church. The RCIA stresses formation in doctrine, liturgy, Church life, and service and involves the larger Church community in welcoming, instructing, helping, and praying for the candidates.

The RCIA has four stages. The first is the *Period of Inquiry* or *Pre-catechumenate*, which may last from several weeks to many months. During this stage candidates are invited to ask questions about the Church, share their own faith stories, and decide whether or not they wish to continue. Those who do continue celebrate the Rite of Becoming a Catechumen and enter the second stage, the *Catechumenate*. This is a more intense period of instruction and introduction to liturgy, faith-life, and service. The Rite of Election, which usually takes place on the First Sunday of Lent, marks the transition between the Catechumenate and the third stage, *Enlightenment and Purification*. This stage covers the season of Lent and includes special liturgical ceremonies at the Lenten Masses, as well as more intense preparation through prayer and study. It climaxes at the Easter Vigil with the sacraments of Initiation—baptism, confirmation, and the holy Eucharist. The final stage of the RCIA is the *Post-baptismal Catechesis (Mystagogia)*. This stage, lasting from Easter to Pentecost, focuses on the mysteries ("mystagogia") of Christ's death and resurrection and helps the newly baptized to develop a deeper understanding of their faith. They now share fully in the Eucharist and are asked to live the gospel in their daily lives and to perform works of service for others.

The RCIA is the process by which nonbaptized candidates are received into the Catholic Church. Baptized members of other Christian denominations who wish to join the Catholic Church are not baptized again, but are received into the Church through penance, profession of faith, confirmation, and the holy Eucharist. The stages of the RCIA may be adapted to meet their needs.

The RCIA can also serve as a focus for ongoing conversion for all members of the Catholic Church. As Catholics see new candidates learning doctrine, they are encouraged to study their faith. As they participate in the liturgical ceremonies welcoming new members, they can renew their own commitment to Christ. As they see the newly baptized begin ministries of service, they are encouraged to serve more generously. And those who act as sponsors, teachers, and "prayer-partners" for the candidates have abundant opportunities for personal growth.

## Baptism and Salvation (C 976–80)

Catholics believe that baptism frees us from sin, unites us to the saving power of Christ's death and resurrection, incorporates us into the Church, and sets us on the path to salvation. Obviously, this is all God's gift and cannot be earned, but baptism is a gift that invites a response. It is birth to a new life of following Jesus. It is not yet salvation fully completed in heaven.

There are some who believe that an individual is saved once and for all by being baptized or by "accepting Jesus as Lord." Such people may ask others, "Have you been saved?" The question assumes "once-saved-always-saved," which is not biblical. Paul urged the Philippians (people who had already been baptized): "Work out your salvation with fear and trembling" (2:12). Paul also wrote, "How much more then, since we are now justified by his blood, will we be saved through him from the wrath" (Romans 5:9).

We might compare salvation to traveling by ship through the waters of this life to the safe haven of eternity. The ship has been built. Christ has done everything necessary by his life, death, and resurrection to bring us to heaven. In this sense salvation has been accomplished (John 3:16). But we must book passage on the ship and be an active part of the crew. We must "work out" our salvation. Jesus warned: "Not everyone who says to me, 'Lord, Lord,' will enter the kingdom of heaven, but only the one who does the will of my Father in heaven" (Matthew 7:21). James asks: "What good is it…if someone says he has faith but does not have works? Can that faith save him?" (2:14; see Matthew 25; 1 Corinthians 15:58; 2 Corinthians 3:18). The Bible shows that it is possible to "jump ship" and choose the wrong destination (1 Corinthians 9:27; 1 Timothy 4:1; 6:10; 6:20-21; 2 Timothy 2:11-13; Hebrews 4:1-11; 6:4-12; 2 Peter 2:20-22).

But we trust that Jesus will see us to our final goal: "I continue my pursuit toward the goal, the prize of God's upward calling, in Christ Jesus" (Philippians 3:14). We trust that Christ, to whom we are united by baptism, will give us salvation and that we will continue to accept it until we arrive in heaven.

### Salvation of the Unbaptized (C 1257–60)

Is baptism necessary for salvation? Jesus said, "No one can enter the kingdom of God without being born of water and Spirit" (John 3:5). Some Christians think this passage means that anyone not actually baptized in water is condemned to hell. But Catholics believe that John 3:5 must be interpreted in the light of Jesus' words at his Ascension: "Whoever believes and is baptized will be saved; whoever does not believe will be condemned" (Mark 16:16). This passage implies that the condemned are those who hear the gospel and refuse to accept it. So the Catholic Church teaches that those who learn of Christ's gospel and culpably reject it are rejecting eternal life. But there are many who are unbaptized through no fault of their own, and the Church believes that they can be saved.

This understanding came very early because some catechumens were martyred before they could be baptized. The Church maintains that those who shed their blood for Christ are joined to him by "baptism of blood." Others desire baptism but die before they can receive it; these people have an explicit "baptism of desire." Still others sincerely try to do what is right but have no opportunity to learn about Christ. These are said to have an implicit "baptism of desire," and the Church teaches that they, too, can be saved.

This teaching has a basis in Scripture. The parable of the Last Judgment in Matthew 25 implies that some will be saved because they ministered to Christ in the poor and hungry, even though they were unaware of his presence. It is also common sense: we do not expect people to follow rules they could not have known. Similarly, God would not expect people to obey the command to be baptized if they had no opportunity to learn about it. People who love and do what is right can be saved. They may not know Christ by name, but they know God, who is love: "Everyone who loves is begotten by God and knows God" (1 John 4:7).

## The Sacrament of Confirmation (C 1285–1321)

In New Testament times the sending of the Holy Spirit was usually associated with baptism. Peter told his hearers at Pentecost, "Repent and be baptized…and you will receive the gift of the holy Spirit" (Acts 2:38). But there are some instances in the New Testament of a special "sending" of the Holy Spirit after baptism. Chapter 8 of Acts of the Apostles tells how the people of Samaria were evangelized and baptized by Philip. When the news reached Jerusalem, the apostles "sent them Peter and John, who went down and prayed for them, that they might receive the holy Spirit, for it had not yet fallen upon any of them; they had only been baptized in the name of the Lord Jesus. Then they laid hands on them and they received the holy Spirit" (8:14-17; see Acts 19). Such passages provided a basis for the celebration of confirmation, a sacramental bestowal of the Holy Spirit apart from baptism, and once infant baptism became common, confirmation began to be celebrated later in life in the Western Church.

At whatever age confirmation is celebrated, it always brings a deepening of baptismal grace. It strengthens our relationship to God the Father as adopted children, draws us nearer to Jesus, and increases the gifts of the Holy Spirit within us. Confirmation intensifies our bond with the Church to help us spread and defend the faith.

The bishop is the ordinary minister of confirmation. Administration of this sacrament by the bishop, a successor of the apostles, emphasizes the fact that the confirmand is being joined more closely to the universal Church. It accentuates the apostolic origin of the Church and its task of giving witness to Christ. However, adults who are baptized or become Catholic through profession of faith are confirmed by the priest who receives them into the Church. Here the priest acts as a representative of the bishop.

The sign used for the bestowal of the Holy Spirit in confirmation is the laying on of hands (Acts 8:14-17) and anointing with sacred chrism. (The use of oil goes back to the anointing of priests, prophets, and kings in the Old Testament.) As the minister anoints the confirmand, he says, "(Name), be sealed with the Gift of the Holy Spirit." The term *sealed* indicates the Church's belief that confirmation bestows a character, a permanent change, as does baptism, so that these sacraments are not repeated. Each candidate has a sponsor who should help by prayer, example, and support. The candidate may choose a "confirmation name" taken from a favorite saint, who is both model and heavenly intercessor.

## Pentecost and the Gifts and Fruits of the Holy Spirit (C 1302–05)

At Pentecost the Holy Spirit came upon the apostles in power, symbolized by fire and a mighty wind (Acts 2), offering friendship and grace to the apostles, allowing them to accomplish what they could not on their own. Confirmation is our Pentecost, when the Spirit offers us grace and friendship.

The effects of the Spirit's grace in our lives have traditionally been expressed as the *gifts* of the Holy Spirit. These are wisdom, understanding, counsel, fortitude, knowledge, piety, and fear of the Lord (Isaiah 11:2; C 1831). The results of the Holy Spirit's friendship are called the *fruits* of the Holy Spirit. They are charity, joy, peace, patience, kindness, goodness, generosity, gentleness, faithfulness, modesty, self-control, and chastity (Galatians 5:22-23; C 1832). These are qualities that can help us lead happy, loving, worthwhile lives, and confirmation makes them available to us. We are no longer alone when we try to be kind, for example; Jesus models kindness for us, and the Spirit helps us to imitate Jesus. What we could not achieve by our own efforts, we can achieve with God's help as kindness becomes a "fruit" of our relationship with the Holy Spirit.

## Confirmation and Friendship With God (C 1303)

Good friends are a source of happiness. Jesus tells us that we can be friends with God (John 15:15). Father, Son, and Spirit love us personally (John 17:23) and want us to be filled with divine life and love. Confirmation is a sacrament that should "confirm" our friendship with God. And while the ceremony of confirmation may take a short time, it can and should have lasting effects.

Two friends might take a vacation together. It may last only a week, but it can strengthen friendship for a lifetime. Confirmation is something like that. It is an event that can deepen our friendship with God and change our whole life for the better. But just as the results of a vacation might depend on how well the friends keep in touch afterward, so the results of confirmation will depend largely on how well we keep in touch with God.

Friends can write, call on the phone, or visit. God won't send us a letter through the postal service, but God has written the Bible for us. God won't call on the phone, but will communicate with us anytime in prayer. God won't ring our doorbell, but will visit with us anytime. Bible, prayer, worship: these are crucial to a life of friendship and intimacy with God. Confirmation offers us God's friendship now and forever!

## Confirmation and Service (C 737–41, 1285)

The coming of the Holy Spirit upon the apostles moved them to do Christ's work. Pentecost got the gospel out from behind locked doors and into the world. Confirmation should help us continue the work of Christ and minister to others. The Holy Spirit offers us gifts like healing and leadership (1 Corinthians 12) for this very reason and helps us understand what we *can* and *should* do.

"Charity begins at home." We begin with our families and acquaintances. When we see someone lonely, hurt, or misunderstood; hungry for food or friendship; imprisoned by fear, worry, or heartache; needing a loving touch or kind word; our response should be what Christ would do if he were in our place.

Next, our parish. We should be a loving community of people who care for one another. Christ asks us to be kind to parishioners by friendliness in the parking lot, words of congratulation after a baptism, presence at a funeral. Most parishes offer many opportunities for service, such as committee work, liturgy, and social-concern organizations.

Then, our world. The Catholic Church provides disaster relief and aid to the needy everywhere in the world. Our gifts to special collections, joined to the gifts of millions of others, can save lives and ease suffering. The Catholic Church joins with other churches to defend the most helpless of human beings, the unborn, and other groups deprived of justice. It is not possible to be actively involved in all social causes, but we can choose at least one organization where we can make a difference through participation, prayer, and monetary gifts.

At home, in our parish, in our world, "if we live in the Spirit, let us also follow the Spirit" (Galatians 5:25).

### Signs of the Spirit's Presence (C 455, 683, 733–36)

An interesting religious phenomenon of the past one hundred years has been the charismatic movement. Reaching many denominations, including the Catholic Church, this movement emphasizes the importance of the Holy Spirit, of the Bible, and of group prayer. It holds that the presence of the Holy Spirit is manifested through gifts like healing, prophecy, and speaking in tongues. These gifts might become evident through the laying on of hands and the "baptism of the Holy Spirit."

Paul's Letters to the Corinthians show that the Church at Corinth was actively charismatic. But other churches founded by Paul were not as charismatic as that of Corinth, and even there not all spoke in tongues (1 Corinthians 12–14). There is room in the Church for a great variety of gifts and ways of worship.

Still, a Catholic might hear about dramatic manifestations of the Holy Spirit and wonder, "Have I received the Holy Spirit?" In 1 Corinthians 12:3 Paul states, "No one can say, 'Jesus is Lord,' except by the holy Spirit." In 1 Corinthians 12:31 to 13:13 he describes love as the greatest gift of the Spirit. Therefore, if we can say with faith that Jesus is Lord, and if we truly love others, we have received the Holy Spirit. Yet we should strive for other spiritual gifts and always try to be more open to the Holy Spirit.

### The Sign of the Cross (C 699, 1235, 2157)

Catholics have the beautiful custom of making the Sign of the Cross with holy water. Blessed water touched to our forehead, heart, and shoulders in the sign of a cross recalls our baptism and the fact that Christ died on the cross to give us new life. The words, "In the name of the Father, and of the Son, and of the Holy Spirit," profess our faith in the Trinity, who unite themselves to us in baptism and confirmation.

The Sign of the Cross should call to mind the great gifts and responsibilities bestowed by these sacraments: "So then you are no longer strangers and sojourners, but you are fellow citizens with the holy ones and members of the household of God, built upon the foundation of the apostles and prophets, with Christ Jesus himself as the capstone. Through him the whole structure is held together and grows into a temple sacred in the Lord; in him you also are being built together into a dwelling place of God in the Spirit" (Ephesians 2:19-22).

## Sacraments and Sacramentals (C 1667–1679)

The Sign of the Cross and holy water are examples of what Catholics call "sacramentals." Sacramentals are sacred signs which resemble the seven sacraments, but are not instituted by Christ and do not convey Christ's grace as the sacraments do. Instead, they are instituted by the Church and symbolize spiritual effects which come about primarily through the prayer of the Church. They open us to God's grace if we use them with faith, just as prayer can open our hearts to God. Sacramentals dispose us to receive the grace of the sacraments and sanctify various occasions in human life.

Most sacramentals are related to the sacraments in some way. Holy water, for example, is blessed water that recalls our baptism. All sacramentals remind us of the goodness of the things God has created. Important sacramentals are prayers of blessing, blessed ashes, bells, candles, crosses, crucifixes, statues, sacred images, medals, oils, palms, and rosaries.

### *Questions for Discussion or Reflection*

What are the happiest memories you have of family rituals? What religious rituals and ceremonies have meant the most to you? Have baptism and confirmation made a difference in your life?

### *Activities*

Place yourself in God's presence and think of your baptism, picturing Jesus as the one baptizing you. Feel the water on your forehead as a sign from Christ that he is filling you with his life. See yourself as the dwelling place of Father, Son, and Holy Spirit. Ask the Holy Spirit to make you more aware of these realities. Think about the fruits of the Holy Spirit listed in this chapter. Which of these qualities do you need most?

Pick out one, think of how Jesus had that quality, and ask the Holy Spirit to help you be more like Jesus.

For a more complete understanding of sacraments and sacramental signs, read *The Privilege of Being Catholic*, Liguori Publications (see Bibliography).

Try to "make a habit" of making the Sign of the Cross devoutly and frequently. You may make it with or without holy water by signing yourself on the forehead, heart, left shoulder and right shoulder as you say, "In the name of the Father, and of the Son, and of the Holy Spirit. Amen."

# CHAPTER NINE
## The Eucharist—
## Christ's Meal and Sacrifice

S oon after children are born they let the world know they are hungry. A baby's cry for food is a dramatic expression of our human need for nourishment. But meals do more than sustain the body. When a mother holds her child to her breast, she satisfies not only the need for food but also the need for closeness and love. Meals bring people together when families gather around the dinner table or teenagers have a pizza or friends enjoy a meal at a restaurant. At meals we remember…an anniversary dinner. We celebrate …a birthday party. We anticipate…a rehearsal meal.

Through baptism, Christ gives us a share in God's life. This life requires spiritual food and drink, which Christ provides at the Eucharist, a meal that nourishes, unites, remembers, celebrates, and anticipates.

### Origins of the Eucharist (C 1322–44)

On the night the Israelites fled from slavery in Egypt, they were told to slaughter a lamb and smear its blood on the doorpost of their homes. This sign would cause the destroying angel to "pass over" their homes when he struck down the firstborn of the Egyptians. They then ate the lamb with unleavened bread and bitter herbs. They were to repeat this meal each year to commemorate their deliverance from slavery (Exodus 12:1-28; Deuteronomy 16:1-8).

The Passover meal became an occasion which fed the Israelites, body and soul. It nourished them and joined them to God and one another. It recalled God's saving deeds and celebrated their freedom. It anticipated the full redemption God would one day bring them through the Messiah.

It was at a Passover celebration that Jesus gathered his apostles for the Last Supper before his Crucifixion. At this meal Jesus "took bread, said the blessing, broke it, and giving it to his disciples said, 'Take and eat; this is my body.' Then he took a cup, gave thanks, and gave it to them, saying, 'Drink from it, all of you, for this is my blood of the covenant, which will be shed on behalf of many for the forgiveness of sins' " (Matthew 26:26-28). The apostles could not have fully understood these words that night. But after Christ's death and resurrection, they realized that in some mysterious way the bread and wine had become Jesus Christ. Christ was their spiritual food and drink!

### "This Is My Body. This Is My Blood." (C 1373–81)

Catholics believe that when Jesus said the words "This is my body....This is my blood," he meant exactly what he said. For Jews, *body* meant the person, and *blood* was the source of life identifiable with the person. So Jesus was saying over the bread and cup, "This is myself," and we believe that the bread and wine truly become the very person of Jesus.

The traditional theological term for this miracle is *transubstantiation*. It means that the "substance" of the bread and wine becomes the "substance" of Christ's body and blood, while the appearances of bread and wine remain. When a priest says the words of Jesus—the words of consecration—over the bread and wine, they still retain the appearance and taste of bread and wine are retained, but the bread and wine become Christ himself, who is then as truly present to us as he was to the apostles.

The New Testament bears witness to the reality of Christ's presence in the Eucharist. The Gospel of John devotes the entire sixth chapter to Jesus as the "Bread of Life." First, Jesus multiplies loaves and fish, a miracle which foreshadows his ability to "multiply his presence" in the Eucharist. Then he walks on water, showing his divine power over nature, a power capable of changing bread into his body. Finally, he urges the crowd to work not "for food that perishes but for the food that endures for eternal life" (6:27). This food is Jesus: "I am the living bread that came down from heaven; whoever eats this bread will live forever; and the bread that I will give is my flesh for the life of the world" (6:51).

When his listeners objected, Jesus declared: "Unless you eat the flesh of the Son of Man and drink his blood, you do not have life within you. Whoever eats my flesh and drinks my blood has eternal life, and I will raise him on the last day. For my flesh is true food and my blood is true drink. Whoever eats my flesh and drinks my blood remains in me and I in him. Just as the living Father sent me and I have life because of the Father, so also the one who feeds on me will have life because of me. This is the bread that came down from heaven. Unlike your ancestors who ate and still died, whoever eats this bread will live forever" (6:53-58).

These words stunned his disciples. "This saying is hard," they said "Who can accept it?" (6:60). Many "returned to their former way of life and no longer accompanied him" (6:66). But Jesus did not call out, "Wait, you misunderstood. I didn't mean that the bread is my body, but that it only *represents* my body." Instead, he asked his apostles, "Do you also want to leave?" Peter answered, "Master, to whom shall we go? You have the words of eternal life. We have come to believe and are convinced that you are the Holy One of God" (6:67-69).

Jesus did not "water down" his statements in the least. They were hard to accept, and Peter did not claim to understand them. He simply accepted them on the authority of Jesus, who had "the words of eternal life."

Paul also believed in the words, "This is my body." After criticizing the Corinthians for their irreverence in receiving the Eucharist, he stated bluntly, "Whoever eats the bread or drinks the cup of the Lord unworthily will have to answer for the body and blood of the Lord" (1 Corinthians 11:27).

Catholics do not claim to understand how bread and wine become Christ's body and blood. We accept, as Peter did, the "words of eternal life." We believe, as Paul did, that the bread and wine are the "body and blood of the Lord." We express our belief that Christ is truly present in the "Blessed Sacrament" in many ways. For example, the Blessed Sacrament is kept in the Church in a tabernacle (from a Latin word meaning "tent"), and we genuflect (bend our knee) as an act of adoration before the Real Presence of Christ.

## The Eucharist as a Meal:
## Jesus Gives Nourishment and Life (C 1382–83)

The Eucharist is a meal, for Christ gave us the Eucharist at a Passover meal, and he chose food and drink as the elements to be changed into himself. The early Christians saw the celebration of

the Eucharist as a meal: Paul called it the "Lord's supper" (1 Corinthians 11:20).

Jesus spoke of the Eucharist as food and drink: "My flesh is
true food, and my blood is true drink" (John 6:55). Jesus wants us to
draw a parallel between what food and drink do for us and what
the Eucharist does for us. Food and drink nourish our body and
become our body. The Eucharist nourishes us, but in this case we
become what we receive. We are transformed into Christ!

Using the imagery of vine and branches, Jesus explains that
we receive life from him: "Remain in me, as I remain in you. Just
as a branch cannot bear fruit on its own unless it remains on the
vine, so neither can you unless you remain in me. I am the vine,
you are the branches" (John 15:4-5). The Eucharist is the means
by which we remain in Christ and receive his life. "Just as the
living Father sent me and I have life because of the Father, so also
the one who feeds on me will have life because of me" (John
6:57). As a healthy branch receives life from the vine, so we can
thrive when we are sustained by the life of Christ.

### The Eucharist as a Meal:
### Jesus Unites Us to Himself (C 1391–95)

Meals join people to one another. When we receive Jesus in the
Eucharist, we are joined to him. Jesus loves us so much that he
died for us. He spoke of us as God's gift to him and prayed that we
might be one with him (John 17:24). Jesus gave us the Eucharist
to unite us to him: "Whoever eats my flesh and drinks my blood
remains in me and I in him" (John 6:56).

To really grasp the meaning of this, we need to think about special
moments of human closeness: parents holding a child, a husband
and wife together, time spent with a best friend. The Eucharist is all
this—and more. The Eucharist is union with Jesus, with the Father,
and with the Holy Spirit, and traditionally Catholics have referred
to the reception of Jesus in the Eucharist as "holy Communion."

### The Eucharist as a Meal:
### Jesus Unites Us to One Another (C 1396–97)

The eucharistic meal joins us not only to Christ but also to one
another. Those who receive Jesus are one because they receive the
one Christ: "The cup of blessing that we bless, is it not a participation in the blood of Christ? The bread that we break, is it not a

participation in the body of Christ? Because the loaf of bread is one, we, though many, are one body, for we all partake of the one loaf" (1 Corinthians 10:16-17). We long for unity and peace. So does Jesus: "I pray…for those who will believe in me…that they may all be one, as you, Father, are in me and I in you, that they also may be in us, that the world may believe that you sent me" (John 17:20-21). He even died "to gather into one the dispersed children of God" (John 11:52), and at every Mass, Jesus brings us together: husband, wife, parents, children, brothers, sisters, friends, strangers.

### The Eucharist as Sacrifice (C 1356–72, 1390)

The Passover meal was also a sacrifice, an offering to the Lord. After the escape from Egypt, Moses sacrificed young bulls at Mount Sinai, splashed some of their blood on God's altar, and sprinkled some on the people. This was a covenant sacrifice expressing the union between God and people. At the time of Jesus, lambs for the Passover were slaughtered at the Temple; their blood was shed and their flesh was eaten with unleavened bread. In this sacrificial meal the Israelites recalled the Exodus and renewed their covenant with God.

With this as background Jesus celebrated the Last Supper. He told his disciples, "No one has greater love than this, to lay down one's life for one's friends" (John 15:13). He made it clear that the Supper was intimately linked to his coming death. He took bread, "broke it" as a sign that his body would be "broken" on the cross, and said, "This is my body, which will be given for you" (Luke 22:19). He took wine and said, "This is my blood of the covenant, which will be shed on behalf of many for the forgiveness of sins" (Matthew 26:28).

This is why Catholics speak of the Eucharist as a sacrifice. Jesus gave his life; he shed his blood for us. In doing so he established a New Covenant between God and us (Hebrews 9:11-15). As the Last Supper anticipated Christ's death on the cross, so each celebration of the Eucharist remembers that death. Paul wrote: "As often as you eat this bread and drink the cup, you proclaim the death of the Lord until he comes" (1 Corinthians 11:26). Catholics believe that the Eucharist makes present the death of Jesus. This does not mean that Christ dies again (Hebrews 7:27). But the Eucharist is a miracle that rolls away the centuries and allows us to stand at the cross of Christ. "The cup of blessing that we bless, is it not a participation in the blood of Christ? The bread that we break, is it not a participation in the body of Christ?" (1 Corinthians 10:16-17).

The "separate consecration" of the bread and wine serves as a reminder that once in history Christ's blood was separated from his body when he died on the cross. When the Eucharist is celebrated today, however, Christ's blood is not separated from his body. The Christ who becomes present at the words of consecration is the risen, glorified Christ. Catholics believe that Christ is fully present in both the bread and wine and that we receive Christ when we communicate under the form of either bread or wine. At the same time we remember that Christ once gave his life for us in the sacrifice of Calvary.

### The Eucharist and Everlasting Life (C 1402–05)

The Jesus who sacrificed his life for us rose from the grave on Easter Sunday, and we receive him in the Eucharist (Philippians 2:5-11). The Eucharist nourishes the life given to us in baptism and confirmation, and that life is eternal (Romans 6:3-11). For these reasons the Eucharist is a special sign of hope that we will live forever.

Jesus wanted this to be so. He said, "Whoever eats my flesh and drinks my blood has eternal life, and I will raise him up on the last day....Whoever eats this bread will live forever" (John 6:54,58). For Paul, the Eucharist was not a memorial to someone dead and gone, but to Christ who is alive and will come again (1 Corinthians 11:26). At every Eucharist we look with confidence to that day when Christ will come to lead us through death to everlasting life.

### The Eucharist Through the Centuries (C 1345)

The first Christians in Jerusalem "devoted themselves to the teaching of the apostles and to the communal life, to the breaking of the bread and to the prayers" (Acts 2:42). This passage may well refer to the prayers, readings, and celebration of the Lord's Supper. Christians certainly developed patterns for the Eucharist very early, for Paul had to correct the Corinthians about abuses at meals they shared in connection with the Lord's Supper (1 Corinthians 11:20-34).

Around A.D. 150 Saint Justin described a celebration of the Eucharist that closely resembled today's Catholic Mass. (*Mass* comes from the Latin word for dismissal from the assembly.) The people gathered together on Sunday, the "Lord's Day," participated in prayers and hymns, and listened to readings from the Old Testament and from the writings of the apostles. Then bread, wine, and water were offered, and the words of Jesus at the Last Supper were prayed by the one presiding. The people received the body and blood of Christ, and holy Communion was brought to the sick. A collection was taken for the poor and needy.

There were many variations around this basic pattern. With the passage of time came a tendency to emphasize the mystery of the Mass as a ceremony performed by the priest and watched by the people. In 1570, after the Council of Trent, Pope Pius V decreed that all Masses in the Roman Catholic Church should be celebrated according to definite rules set up in the *Roman Missal*. For almost four centuries Mass was prayed in Latin from this missal.

By the middle of the twentieth century, a movement for liturgical renewal encouraged more participation on the part of the congregation, along patterns observed in the early days of the Church. Since Vatican II, Mass has been celebrated in the language of the people, and participation by the congregation and by ministers such as lectors and eucharistic ministers has become common.

## Liturgy of the Word and Liturgy of the Eucharist (C 1066–75, 1346–55)

*Liturgy* means "work," and the liturgy is certainly one of the most important works of the Church. Liturgy embraces all official worship of the Church, but it is often used to refer specifically to the Mass. Within the Mass itself there are two main divisions—the Liturgy of the Word and the Liturgy of the Eucharist.

The Liturgy of the Word begins with the Sign of the Cross and greetings exchanged by priest and people. There is a brief pause to call to mind our sins and an act of sorrow. On Sundays (and other special days) we may pray the Glory, a hymn of praise. After the priest offers a prayer, the Scriptures are read. The usual pattern for Sundays and special feasts is a first reading from the Old

Testament, a responsorial psalm, a second reading from a New Testament book, an acclamation verse, and a reading from a gospel. On weekdays, before the gospel there is only one reading from either the Old or New Testament, followed by the responsorial psalm. Then a homily is given, applying the readings to everyday life. On Sundays and major feasts the congregation professes its faith by praying the Nicene Creed. The Liturgy of the Word closes with the prayer of the faithful, in which we place our needs before God.

The Liturgy of the Eucharist begins when the offerings of the community and the bread and wine are brought to the altar. These are presented to God by the priest, who then washes his hands as a sign of our need for purification. After a prayer over the gifts, and one said by priest and congregation asking God to accept the sacrifice, we move to the eucharistic prayer. Its introduction is called the preface, chosen from many options to suit the occasion. There are nine different eucharistic prayers, including three for children's Masses and two for reconciliation. All include the words used by Jesus (the "Consecration") at the Last Supper, by which the bread and wine become Christ. The eucharistic prayer concludes with the great amen, proclaimed by the congregation as its "yes" to all that has gone before. We then recite the Our Father, which is followed by a prayer for deliverance from evil and a prayer for peace. Remembering that we must be at peace with one another before we can approach God's altar (Matthew 5:23), we offer a sign of peace. Those taking holy Communion receive Christ under the sign of bread or both bread and wine. After Communion there is time for quiet reflection and thanksgiving. The Mass draws to a close as the priest says a prayer, then blesses and dismisses the congregation.

Within this general structure of the Mass, there are many options. People just starting to attend Mass can become familiar with it by requesting one of the missalettes available at many churches. Some may feel self-conscious and fearful of making a blunder at Mass; a good rule is to observe what others are doing, whether standing, sitting, or kneeling, then imitate them.

Hymns may be sung at Mass, and many parts of the Mass may be sung by priest and congregation. "Singing is praying twice," according to Saint Augustine, with words and melody. Singing praises God and brings people together.

## Guidelines for Receiving Communion
## (C 1384–90, 1398–1401)

From the earliest days of the Church, receiving the Lord in holy Communion was seen as a sign of unity with the Church. Those preparing to join the Church did not receive Communion until they were baptized and confirmed at the Easter Vigil. Today Communion signifies unity with the Church in sacramental life, belief, and morals. This is expressed in guidelines for the reception of holy Communion issued by the National Conference of Catholic Bishops on November 8, 1986:

> *For Catholics:* Catholics fully participate in the celebration of the Eucharist when they receive Holy Communion in fulfillment of Christ's command to eat His Body and drink His Blood. In order to be properly disposed to receive Communion, communicants should not be conscious of grave sin, have fasted for an hour, and seek to live in charity and love with their neighbors. Persons conscious of grave sin must first be reconciled with God and the Church through the sacrament of penance....

> *For Other Christians:* We welcome to this celebration of the Eucharist those Christians who are not fully united with us. It is a consequence of the sad divisions in Christianity that we cannot extend to them a general invitation to receive Communion. Catholics believe that the Eucharist is an action of the celebrating community signifying a oneness in faith, life and worship of the community. Reception of the Eucharist by Christians not fully united with us would imply a oneness which does not yet exist and for which we must all pray (*Origins*, January 15, 1987, Vol. 16, No. 31, p. 554).

## The Eucharist and the Liturgical Year (C 1163–73)

We celebrate great events each year. We have holidays to recall events like the birth of our nation. We anticipate special days with decorations, parties, and family traditions. We may relive certain events by re-creating battles and sponsoring pageants. Between holidays, life returns to its ordinary routine.

The "liturgical year" is the Church's way of celebrating and reliving the great events of our salvation. Each year follows a pattern, and the readings and prayers for Mass have been organized to fit into it. The liturgical year begins with Advent, four weeks of preparation for Christmas. On the twenty-fifth of December we observe the birthday of Christ and reflect on the Incarnation. After Christmas other feasts prolong the celebration: Holy Family Sunday, the Solemnity of Mary, Mother of God (New Year's Day), Epiphany, and the Baptism of the Lord.

There follows a period of Ordinary Time, the length of which depends on the date of Easter. The Lenten preparation for Easter begins on Ash Wednesday, when we are marked with ashes on our foreheads as a sign of willingness to do penance and reform our lives. As catechumens make final preparations for baptism, all Catholics are challenged during Lent to die to sin and rise to new life. Lent ends at the sacred triduum, three days which relive the events of the first Holy Thursday, Good Friday, and Holy Saturday. We celebrate the Resurrection with the Easter Vigil and the Masses of Easter, the greatest feast of the Church year. Easter season continues through Ascension Thursday (forty days after Easter) and ends on Pentecost Sunday (ten days after Ascension).

Ordinary Time resumes the day after Pentecost, but the next two Sundays commemorate the Trinity and the Body and Blood of Christ. Ordinary Time continues through the last Sunday of the liturgical year, the Solemnity of Christ the King, after which the First Sunday of Advent starts another cycle again.

Christ is free of the limits of space and time and relives with us the events of his life through the liturgical year. Through Scripture readings and prayers appropriate to the events being celebrated, God speaks to us. We respond by participating in the liturgy, and so are joined to the birth, life, dying, and rising of Christ, as once again Jesus walks the pathways of our world.

All through the liturgical year, special place is given to Sunday, observed as the Lord's Day because Christ rose on the first day of the week. Most major liturgical observances occur on Sunday, but there are also special feasts in the liturgical year called holy days of obligation. In the United States we observe six: Christmas on the twenty-fifth of December; Solemnity of Mary, Mother of God on the first of January; Ascension Thursday, Mary's Assumption on the fifteenth of August; All Saints' Day on the first of

November; and the Immaculate Conception on the eighth of December.

There is a cycle of Scripture readings at Mass found in the book called the *Lectionary* following a three-year pattern for Sundays and a two-year pattern for weekdays. Prayers found in the altar book, the *Sacramentary*, are repeated annually.

Throughout the liturgical year, the Catholic Church observes feast days in honor of the saints. As we remember their lives in special prayers at Mass and ask them to pray for us, we heed the biblical command: "Remember your leaders who spoke the word of God to you. Consider the outcome of their way of life and imitate their faith" (Hebrews 13:7).

## The Sunday Obligation (C 1166–67, 1389)

Sundays are special. Christians in New Testament times met for the breaking of the bread on the first day of the week (Acts 20:7) because this was the day Christ rose from the grave. They thus obeyed the third commandment: "Keep holy the Lord's day." Jesus had said, "Do this in remembrance of me," and they hastened to do what the Lord had asked.

As time passed, some Christians fell away. The author of the Letter to the Hebrews urged his readers to be faithful: "We should not stay away from our assembly, as is the custom of some, but encourage one another, and this all the more as you see the day drawing near" (10:25). Worthy participation in the Eucharist is essential to life in Christ, as Paul noted (1 Corinthians 11:29-30). In times of persecution, Christians risked their lives to share the Eucharist. For them, it was a great privilege to be invited to the Lord's Supper.

Today, almost two thousand years later, the Catholic Church maintains its belief in the importance of the Eucharist. Surely, we ought not say "No, thank you" to the Lord's own invitation to "do this in remembrance" of him, and so the Church points out the necessity of the Eucharist by requiring that we attend Mass on Sundays and holy days. (In a change recommended by the American Bishops in 1991 and approved by Rome in 1992, when the Solemnity of Mary, the Assumption of Mary, and All Saints' Day fall on a Saturday or a Monday, Mass attendance is not required, though it is certainly encouraged. The obligation to attend Mass remains on the Ascension, Immaculate Conception, and Christmas, regardless of the day of the week). Except when we are prevented from sharing in the Mass by illness or responsibilities such as caring for the sick, we should attend Mass as gladly as we would respond to any personal invitation from Jesus himself.

All at Mass have a unique part to play in offering their lives to the Father in union with Christ's offering of his life on the cross. All can bring to Mass the events of the past week and their hopes for the week ahead. Our offering is incomplete when some believers are absent. Further, we go to Mass to be with others. Attending Mass is not like attending a movie, where many happen to be together to see the same show. It is rather like a family reunion, which we attend precisely to meet others and to express and strengthen our unity. When any Catholic is missing, our family reunion in Christ is less than it should be.

On Sundays we should also refrain from work or business that would keep us from the worship and attention owed to God. Sunday should be a day of joy, of celebration, of relaxation. It should be a time to find God in our family, in others, and in the beauty of creation.

## Sight, Scent, Sound, Touch, and Taste (C 1153–58, 1179–86)

Jesus loved the world he entered through the Incarnation. His parables are full of sight, scent, sound, touch, and taste. He obviously believed that truth, beauty, and grace can be conveyed through created things. In Catholic liturgy material things are used to express spiritual realities, and Catholic churches are typically full of sights, scents, sounds, and things to touch and taste.

Colors are used in vestments and altar adornments to express various meanings. Purple and violet signify anticipation, purification, or penance, and are used in Advent and Lent. Red is the color of blood and symbolizes the supreme sacrifice of life given for others; it is used for Passion Sunday, Good Friday, and the feasts of martyrs. Red is also the color of fire and is used on Pentecost Sunday. White expresses joy, purity, and eternal life; it is used for most feasts of our Lord, for the seasons of Christmas and Easter, for funerals, for feasts of saints, and for angels. Green, the color of growing things, is symbolic of life and the vitality of faith, hope, and love. It is used for Ordinary Time. Whatever their color, the chasuble (outer vestment) and stole (strip of cloth) worn by the priest signify that Christ is truly present at Mass as our High Priest.

Anyone attending Mass will see the crucifix, vessels containing bread and wine, candles, statues, stained-glass windows, familiar faces, flowers, and many other sights which delight the senses, teach the mind, and warm the heart.

Scent enhances worship. Incense is used to signify our adoration of God and our hope that our prayer will rise up as does the smoke and odor of incense (Psalm 141:1-2; Revelation 5:8). Flowers add the beauty of scent, as well as of sight.

Sound is a part of worship. Bells are rung to summon the congregation, announce a death, or proclaim our joy. Musical instruments express every human emotion and nuance of worship. Prayers are said and hymns are sung.

As many Catholics enter a church, they touch their fingers to holy water and sign themselves with the cross. Touch becomes a way for us to reach out to others at the sign of peace and other times. Kneeling and standing and sitting are postures for worship, prayer, listening, and reflection.

"Learn to savor how good the LORD is" exhorted the psalmist (34:9). We experience the truth of this when we receive the Lord in holy Communion. The taste of bread, the staff of life, tells us of the eternal life Christ gives in the Eucharist. The taste of wine, that gladdens our hearts (Psalm 104:15), opens our minds and hearts to the joy and peace that only Christ can give.

God loves the world. We Catholics believe this and, following Jesus, we find ways to worship our God and to receive blessings from God's hands in sight, scent, sound, touch, and taste. We thus open our lives to the central reality of the Eucharist: Jesus Christ, the Word-made-flesh.

### All I Want Is to Know Christ (C 1406–19)

Some people say they get nothing out of Mass, that the sermons are boring, and that churchgoers are no better than anyone else. They should recall that Jesus' own townspeople rejected him because they didn't like his sermon and because he seemed so ordinary (Luke 4:16-30). Without denying the importance of good sermons and the need to strive for holiness, we must remember that Christ does not need perfect preachers to touch our hearts and that he came to save sinners.

The Mass does not depend on any one thing for its value or meaning. There are prayers and Scripture readings which never lose their power as God's Word. There are the avenues of sight, scent, sound, touch, and taste by which we can draw closer to heaven. There is always the Lord. The church may be humble, the singing off-key, the preacher ordinary. But at Christ's words, "This is my body," all limitations are stripped away and we stand in the very presence of God. It is, above all, at the Eucharist that we make Paul's wish our own: "All I want is to know Christ and to experience the power of his resurrection, to share in his sufferings and become like him in his death, in the hope that I myself will be raised from death to life" (Philippians 3:10-11, *Good News Bible*).

### *Questions for Discussion or Reflection*

Why do you think people have risked their lives to smuggle bread and wine into concentrations camps to celebrate the Eucharist? Some Protestant denominations have an "altar call," inviting people to come to the altar and accept Jesus as Savior. How is holy Communion like an altar call? and much more besides? When you attend Mass, you are standing at Calvary near the cross of Jesus. Compare your attitude with the attitudes of those who witnessed Christ's death on Calvary. Is your attitude like that of Mary, of the soldiers, of the Jewish leaders, or of indifferent passers-by?

### *Activities*

If you find Mass boring, it may be that you are coming because you "have to" or only to "get something" out of Mass. Try coming because you want to give something. Come to give God your thanks and worship. Come to give Jesus your love and friendship. Come to give prayers for others, a smile to others, a helping hand to the elderly. Come to give a part of your income to the work of the Church. Come to give God all the events of your past week and your hopes and plans for the next week. If you come to church to give, Mass will never be boring!

# CHAPTER TEN
## Reconciliation—Jesus Forgives

"Nothing is new under the sun" (Ecclesiastes 1:9). We constantly rediscover old truths. One truth rediscovered in our time is that "confession is good for the soul." Psychiatry and psychology are relatively new sciences, but they frequently depend on the old art of listening to problems, which often include guilt. Guilt can eat away at people, causing physical and emotional ills, but when it is brought to the surface, healing begins. Confession is good for the soul.

Jesus knew this well. He came to call sinners (Mark 2:17); he welcomed them and ate with them (Luke 15:2). He listened to people unburden themselves of guilt. He spoke words of healing: "Your sins are forgiven" (Mark 2:5).

### The Reality of Sin (C 1425–26)

Karl Menninger, a psychiatrist, wrote a book titled *Whatever Became of Sin?* In it he said that people worry about crime, violence, terrorism, war, cheating, unethical conduct, and a host of other problems, but still avoid talk of sin. Yet sin exists and should be spelled "s-I-n," for it means that I set myself and my choices against those of God and others. Sin is pride and self-centeredness.

"Nothing is new under the sun." The Bible tells us how God created human beings and invited them to choose what is right. Instead, Adam and Eve ate from the "tree of knowledge of good and bad." In effect, they said to God, "We will decide what is right and wrong." They set their choices against God's, and sin entered the world, alienating people from God, from one another, and from creation: Adam and Eve hid from God, blamed each other, and felt pain and suffering. And over everything fell the dark shadow of death (Genesis 2–3).

Adam and Eve are all those who make sinful choices and live in a world which is less than paradise because it is limited by the sins of countless generations. "All have sinned and are deprived of the glory of God" (Romans 3:23).

Repeatedly, the world has been overwhelmed by sin, nations destroyed by war, and societies undermined by lust. Sin immerses people in a flood of self-inflicted evil, as the story of Noah illustrates (Genesis 6–9).

What is true for society is true for us as individuals. When we oppose the will of God and choose our way over God's, we inevitably suffer. Through sin, we lose peace of mind and find instead the anguish of guilt and self-reproach.

## The Mercy and Forgiveness of God (C 1440–42)

Sin is a flood of evil from which we can be rescued only by the ark of God's forgiveness. The good news of the Bible is that forgiveness is available, for God is "gracious and merciful, slow to anger and of great kindness" (Psalm 145:8). The Israelites experienced that forgiveness, even for crimes as great as those of David, who murdered a loyal soldier and stole his wife (2 Samuel 11–12). Again and again they turned from God. Again and again overwhelmed by the consequences of sin, they returned to God for mercy and forgiveness.

But the human race as a whole was unresponsive to God's law and call for repentance. We were held captive by sin (Romans 1–3), but God did not abandon us. Rather, God revealed great mercy: "When the fullness of time had come, God sent his Son, born of a woman, born under the law, to ransom those under the law, so that we might receive adoption" (Galatians 4:4-5).

## Jesus, Messenger of God's Mercy and Forgiveness (C 1427–33)

The message of Jesus presumed the existence of sin and the opportunity for forgiveness: "This is the time of fulfillment. The kingdom of God is at hand. Repent, and believe in the gospel" (Mark 1:15). Whereas many of Israel's religious leaders shunned sinners, Jesus associated with them and extended God's mercy to them with remarkable sympathy, sensitivity, and understanding.

There was the sinful woman who knelt before Jesus while he was dining at the house of Simon the Pharisee. She bathed Jesus' feet with her tears, wiped them with her hair, and anointed them with ointment. This act of contrition drew scorn from the Pharisees, but Jesus praised her great love. He spoke the words she wanted so much to hear: "Your sins are forgiven....Go in peace" (Luke 7:48,50).

There was the tax collector, Zacchaeus (Luke 19:1-10), who heard that the famous teacher, Jesus, was coming to Jericho. Unhappy in his wealthy isolation, he must have longed for the mercy and understanding of Jesus. Small of stature, he could not see Jesus because of the crowds, so he climbed a tree. Jesus looked into his heart and saw a need for forgiveness and a desire to change. He promptly invited himself to Zacchaeus' home. Some grumbled, saying, "He has gone to stay at the house of a sinner." But Zacchaeus knew that Jesus was offering him a new life. He stood his ground and said, "Behold, half of my possessions, Lord, I shall give to the poor, and if I have extorted anything from anyone I shall repay it four times over." Jesus responded, "Today salvation has come to this house...for the Son of Man has come to seek and to save what was lost." And so a man imprisoned by greed was set free by the love, understanding, and mercy of Jesus (Luke 19:1-10).

The full extent of Christ's capacity for forgiveness was shown as he died on the cross. He prayed even for those who had crucified him: "Father, forgive them, they know not what they do" (Luke 23:34). Then one of the criminals nailed beside him asked for mercy: "Jesus, remember me when you come into your kingdom." Jesus assured him of pardon: "Amen, I say to you, today you will be with me in Paradise" (Luke 23:42-43).

These people, and so many others, experienced interaction with God which had previously been impossible. They looked into God's eyes and saw sympathy and understanding, stood in God's presence and shared their sorrow and shame. They heard God say, "Your sins are forgiven. Go in peace."

## Parables of Pardon and Peace (C 1439)

Jesus showed by word and action that God is more merciful than we ever imagined. Lest we still underestimate God's readiness to forgive, Jesus described it in parables. The most beautiful of these are found in Luke's Gospel.

There is the parable of the Lost Sheep. The shepherd searches until he finds the sheep, "sets it on his shoulders with great joy and, upon his arrival home, he calls together his friends and neighbors and says to them, 'Rejoice with me because I have found my lost sheep'" (Luke 15:5-6).

Next follows the parable of the Lost Coin. A woman loses a coin. She searches until she finds it, then calls friends in to celebrate (Luke 15:8-10).

Finally, Jesus tells the parable of the Prodigal Son. A young man insolently asks his father for his inheritance, leaves, and squanders everything. Reduced to destitution, he decides to return home, asking only to be allowed back as a servant. His father sees him coming, rushes out to embrace him, and welcomes him back with a magnificent party (Luke 15:11-32).

These three parables convey the same message: the unbelievable love and mercy of God. In each parable there is a party even though there is really no reason for it. Sheep are always wandering off. A shepherd throwing a party because he found one sheep would be thought strange. The same could be said for a woman who calls friends to celebrate because she found a misplaced coin. And any Jewish father who killed a fatted calf because an ungrateful son came crawling back in desperate need would be judged insane. That is precisely the point! God is so merciful that by human standards God is "off the scale." We might suppose that one sinner out of billions of people on the globe couldn't possibly matter to God. On the contrary, there is "rejoicing among the angels of God over one sinner who repents" (Luke 15:10).

## Christ Shares With His Church
## the Power to Forgive (C 979–87, 1420–26, 1441–45)

Christ offered forgiveness and taught us about God's mercy. Then he made the supreme sacrifice of love, giving his life for us. "For Christ, while we were still helpless, yet died at the appointed time for the ungodly. Indeed, only with difficulty does one die for a just person....But God proves his love for us in that while we were still sinners Christ died for us" (Romans 5:6-8).

In light of all this it would have been surprising if Jesus had not given his Church a sacrament for the forgiveness of sins. The Catholic Church believes that Jesus did so in the sacrament of penance, known also as reconciliation or confession.

## The Sacrament of Penance (C 1446–60)

The gift of forgiveness was the very first gift made by Jesus to his apostles after the Resurrection: "On the evening of that first day of the week, when the doors were locked, where the disciples were, for fear of the Jews, Jesus came and stood in their midst and said to them, 'Peace be with you.' When he had said this, he showed them his hands and his side. The disciples rejoiced when they saw the Lord. [Jesus] said to them again, 'Peace be with you. As the Father has sent me, so I send you.' And when he had said this, he breathed on them and said to them, 'Receive the holy Spirit. Whose sins you forgive are forgiven them, and whose sins you retain are retained'" (John 20:19-23).

Scripture scholars debate about whether these words refer to baptism, to penance, or to both. But they certainly convey the belief of the first Christians that Jesus had entrusted to them his mission to forgive sins, and they shared his forgiveness in many ways: baptism, Eucharist, anointing, prayer, and the sacrament of penance.

The sacrament of penance has undergone many developments. The earliest evidence indicates that those who sinned after baptism were reconciled to the Church through the bishop. Some heretical groups denied that serious sins such as adultery, apostasy, and murder could be forgiven, but this opinion was condemned by the Council of Nicea in 325, which taught that Christ pardons all repentant sinners. At this time, as a matter of fact, the sacrament of penance was used primarily for the forgiveness of serious sins. Penitents would go through a long period of public penance, particularly in Lent, and were then reconciled to the Church at Easter. In the sixth century, through the influence of Irish monks, penance became generally available for less serious sins, and private penitential practices replaced the rigorous discipline of earlier times.

In the twelfth century the theology of penance took on dimensions that shaped usage of the sacrament to our own day. Theologians explained that penance included contrition (sorrow and conversion), confession of sins to a priest, satisfaction (doing penance for one's sins and making up for any harm caused by those sins), and absolution (declaration of forgiveness) by a priest. These four elements were affirmed by the Council of Trent in

1551 after the sacraments were questioned by Protestants. By the twentieth century it was common for Catholics to go to confession quite frequently, usually following a set pattern for the sacrament.

Vatican II called for a revision of penance in order to express more clearly its nature and effects. A new Rite of Reconciliation was established in 1974. It expanded the use of Scripture, emphasized the role of the priest as a healer in Christ's name, pointed out the importance of the Church in reconciling us with God, and offered options for the reception of the sacrament.

The first option is individual reception of the sacrament of penance, either behind a screen or face to face. The second is a communal service, where many people gather to pray and prepare for the sacrament, and then have the opportunity for individual confession of sins. The third option, general confession and absolution, is used in emergency situations where enough priests are not available for individual confessions. ("General confession" means that people say a prayer of sorrow together, not that they confess personal sins publicly; Catholics are never required to confess personal sins publicly.)

## Preparing for the Sacrament of Penance (C 1454)

The sacrament of penance is a meeting with Christ. We should begin preparation for it by praying for the faith to be fully aware of Christ's presence. We should pray also for the grace to see our lives as Christ does, recognize our sins, understand how they offend God, and then confess them honestly.

Next we examine our conscience. There are pamphlets and books available for this, or the following guide may be used. All unconfessed serious (mortal) sins should be told. "Mortal sins" are those that involve serious matter and are committed with full knowledge and full consent of the will. Less serious sins are called venial sins. (More will be said about this in chapter fourteen). We should look for our most significant venial sins, pick out two or three, and confess them. We should not make a "grocery list" of sins, but look into the reasons why we fail and into the attitudes behind our sins.

**An Examination of Conscience**
**Based on the Ten Commandments (C 2052–57)**
*(See Exodus 20:1-20 and Deuteronomy 5:1-21.)*

1. **I am the Lord your God. You shall not have other gods besides me.** Do I think about God and put God first in my life? Do I set aside time each day for worship, prayer, and Bible reading? Do I nourish the virtues of faith, hope, and love by study and prayer? Am I faithful to the promises I have made to God at baptism, confirmation, and choice of vocation? Am I superstitious? Am I involved in astrology, magic, or new-age practices? Do I make a false god of possessions, pleasure, or power? Am I too materialistic? Am I arrogant or self-centered?

2. **You shall not take the name of the Lord your God in vain.** Do I use God's name reverently? Do I reverence God the Father as my Creator, Jesus as my Savior, the Holy Spirit as my Helper? Do I profess my faith in them to family, friends, and others? Do I blaspheme or make false oaths? Do I sin by cursing, swearing, or careless use of God's name?

3. **Remember to keep holy the Lord's day.** Do I worship God faithfully at Sunday Mass, holy days, and other times? Do I do anything special—like prayer, Bible reading, charitable deeds, and family time—to make Sunday the "Lord's Day"? Do I make Sunday a day of rest and relaxation? Have I done my share for my parish through volunteer service?

4. **Honor your father and your mother.** Do I respect and care for my parents and other members of my family? Do I find ways to show my love for them and tell them I love them? Do I show gratitude to them? Do I fulfill my responsibilities and do my share of work at home? Do I pray with members of my family? If a parent, do I offer spiritual leadership and see to the religious instruction of my children? Do I show proper respect to those in authority? Do I fulfill my obligations to my country by paying just taxes, exercising the right

to vote, and defending my country? Have I disobeyed those who have authority over me? Have I shirked my responsibilities to family or society?

5. **You shall not kill.** Do I respect and revere human life as a gift from God from conception through old age? Have I reached out to the sick, elderly, and lonely? Do I pray and work for peace and justice? Am I courteous? Have I ever injured anyone? Have I taken part in an abortion? Have I cooperated in any way in procedures of direct euthanasia? Have I injured myself through alcohol, drugs, smoking, overeating, or excessive dieting? Have I harmed others by hatred, unjust anger, resentment, or unwillingness to forgive? Have I given scandal to others, particularly to the young or those under my authority? Do I belittle or discourage others? Am I prejudiced?

6. **You shall not commit adultery.** Have I been pure in words and actions? Does my clothing reflect the standards of Christ? Have I treated members of the opposite sex with respect and dignity? Have I tried to show love and friendship to members of my family, to friends, and to acquaintances? Have I consciously tried to strengthen marriages and to promote Christlike attitudes toward marriage? Have I sinned by adultery, fornication, masturbation, or other impure actions? Have I indulged in pornographic movies, television, reading, or other entertainments that offend against decency?

7. **You shall not steal.** Have I given an honest day's work for my wages? Have I been fair to employees? Have I shown respect for the property of others? Have I been faithful in keeping promises and contracts? Have I been generous in my gifts to the poor and to the Church? Do I let Christ's teachings guide me in business matters? Have I stolen anything, been dishonest, or cheated? Have I made reparation for any injustice committed against others? Have I harmed myself, my family, or others by excessive gambling?

8. **You shall not bear false witness against your neighbor.** Have I consciously tried to speak well of others? Have I been truthful? Have I harmed others by false

witness or perjury? Have I told lies, deceiving those who had a right to the truth? Have I betrayed secrets? Have I gossiped? Have I judged others rashly? Have I flattered others? Have I boasted or bragged?

9. **You shall not covet your neighbor's wife.** Have I been holy in my thoughts, a "temple of the Holy Spirit"? Have I tried to live by the beatitude which promises that the pure of heart shall see God? Do I have a healthy respect for modesty and for purity of heart? Have I indulged in impure thoughts and desires? Have I led others into sexual sin?

10. **You shall not covet your neighbor's goods.** Have I made heaven my true goal in life and focused my hopes on God? Do I realize that perfect happiness can come only from seeing God face to face in heaven? Do I appreciate God's free gifts, such as the beauties of nature? Have I been generous with my time, talents, and treasure? Am I greedy or avaricious? Have I been envious or jealous of others? Do I make myself and others unhappy by my complaints, my self-pity, or my selfishness?

## Celebrating the Sacrament of Penance (C 1480–84)

In most Catholic churches there are reconciliation rooms furnished with a kneeler, screen, and chairs. The penitent has a choice of kneeling behind the screen and confessing anonymously or sitting in a chair and confessing face to face. Reconciliation is celebrated as follows:

1. **Reception of the penitent.** After the penitent exchanges greetings with the priest, the two make the Sign of the Cross. The priest says a short prayer to which the penitent responds, "Amen."

2. **Reading of God's Word.** The priest may read or recite a brief passage of Scripture, or the penitent may do so.

3. **Confession of sins.** The penitent tells how long it has been since the last confession (an approximation is sufficient) and confesses sins for which forgiveness is needed. The priest may offer words of advice or encouragement, then gives an act of penance.

4. **Prayer of penitent and absolution.** The penitent expresses sorrow through any act of contrition (for example, "Jesus, I am sorry for all my sins. Have mercy on me"). The priest says the prayer of absolution: "God the Father of mercies, through the death and Resurrection of his Son, has reconciled the world to himself and sent the Holy Spirit among us for the forgiveness of sins. Through the ministry of the Church, may God give you pardon and peace, and I absolve you from your sins in the name of the Father, and of the Son, and of the Holy Spirit." The penitent responds, "Amen."

5. **Proclamation of praise of God and dismissal.** The priest says, "Give thanks to the Lord, for he is good." The penitent answers, "His mercy endures forever." The priest closes with a short blessing or prayer.

After confession, we should thank God for the grace of the sacrament and carry out the penance given us by the priest. The penance may consist of prayer, service, self-denial, or voluntary acceptance of necessary suffering. It helps make up for any harm done by our sin, and it more closely joins us to Jesus, who suffered for us.

In communal services, people gather at church at a scheduled time. The ceremony may begin with a song. There are prayers and Scripture readings, examination of conscience, an act of sorrow, then individual confessions and absolution. People may remain after confession for a closing prayer, blessing, and hymn. Such celebrations remind us that sin has a communal dimension; any sin, even the most private, harms the Church, just as a wound to any part of the body injures the whole person. Communal services of penance also let people pray with and for one another, allowing Christ to touch hearts in remarkable ways.

## The Value of Confession (C 1434–39, 1468–79)

It is one thing to know how to go to confession. It is another thing to go! Most people find it hard to admit guilt, and they ask, "Why must I confess my sins to another human being? Why can't I confess them directly to God?"

We can and should confess directly to God as soon as we are aware that we have committed any sin, large or small. The sacrament of penance is regarded as absolutely necessary by the Church only when a Catholic has committed a serious sin and wishes to receive the Eucharist. Since Catholics are required, as a minimum, to receive Communion at least once during the Easter season (Ash Wednesday to Trinity Sunday), penance is necessary then for those in serious sin. Those free of serious sin are not required to go to confession.

Hopefully, however, we who are followers of Jesus will look beyond what we *must* do to what we *should* do. Jesus has given the sacrament of penance to us. Our response ought not be, "Must I accept your gift?" Rather, it should be, "Thank you, Lord. How can I best make use of your gift?"

We will make the best use of penance when we appreciate its tremendous benefits. The most important value of this sacrament is that it allows us to meet Christ and receive his word that our sins are forgiven.

Second, there is value in the very act of admitting our guilt to another human being. When guilt is brought to the surface, it begins to lose its power to hurt. The old phrase "skeleton in the closet" is indicative of the harm which hidden guilt can do. Some of the most successful self-help groups, like Alcoholics Anonymous, believe that we must tell our failings to another. The fourth and fifth of the Twelve Steps in A.A. are: "We made a searching and fearless moral inventory of ourselves" and "We admitted to God, to ourselves, and to another human being the exact nature of our wrongs." (The Fourth and Fifth Steps from the Twelve Steps are reprinted for adaptation with permission of Alcoholics Anonymous World Services, Inc.) Common sense teaches the same thing. A friend may come to us and say, "Something is bothering me. I feel so guilty and just don't know what to do about it." Our first response will probably be, "Would you like to talk about it?" In penance we can honestly and openly admit our sins to the priest, and we will be better for it. "Therefore, confess your sins to one another and pray for one another, that you may be healed" (James 5:16).

Third, there is value in hearing that we are forgiven. When we apologize to someone, we need to hear our apology accepted. "I am sorry." "I forgive you." If the person to whom we apologize says nothing, we can't be sure that we have been forgiven. When we apologize to God for our sins, no voice booms from the sky to say that we are forgiven. How does God accept our apology and tell us, "I forgive you"? Through the sacrament of penance! Jesus told the apostles: "Whose sins you forgive are forgiven them" (John 20:23).

Fourth, confession helps us when we *have* sinned seriously. People can do shameful things, then think, "If others knew me as I really am, they could not accept me." Those who fear that no one could accept them put themselves at the bottom of the human race. But when a sinner confesses, then is accepted and assured of God's pardon, that sinner begins to realize: "Yes, I have done evil things, but I am not evil. If the confessor and God accept me, then I can accept myself as a good person who has done evil, but now wishes to turn away from sin."

Fifth, confession helps us when we have *not* sinned seriously. Christ offers us his grace each time we confess even less serious sins, strengthening us in the love of God. Confession also sharpens our spiritual vision. We can drift along in life, spiritually lazy, failing to see "little" sins like selfishness, gossip, and impatience. People who use penance faithfully are encouraged to examine their consciences, take stock of their failings, and look to God for the forgiveness and help God alone can give. (People who feel they have no need of confession might say to members of their family: "I'd go to confession, but I can't remember any faults. Can you think of any I might have?" Help will be forthcoming!)

Sixth, penance helps us realize that while sin may be classified as "serious" and "less serious," it is never trivial. Sin is always an offense against God. Sin crucified our Savior. Penance reminds us that sin must not be taken lightly.

Seventh, confession brings out the fact that sin is not just a personal matter between me and God. The Church is the Body of Christ, so every sin against Christ offends the Church, and reconciliation with Christ requires reconciliation with the Church. Confession allows this because the priest is a representative of the Church. Further, all churches believe that we must be baptized by another; we do not baptize ourselves. The Catholic Church believes that we must be reconciled by another; we do not absolve ourselves!

Eighth, we will appreciate the sacrament of penance more if we place it in the context of the many penitential practices offered us by the Church. Prayer, fasting, almsgiving, the Bible, the Eucharist, the season of Lent, the designation of Friday as a day honoring Christ's Passion, and indulgences (see page 66) help us to overcome sin and the "temporal punishment" due to sin. To explain...

Unrepented mortal sins, of course, subject a person to the eternal punishment of hell. Mortal sins which have been forgiven, as well as venial sins, do not carry the penalty of hell, but they have other harmful consequences. They lessen our love of God and attach us to imperfections. Purification from these consequences is known as the "temporal punishment" due to sin. Such purification must take place here on earth or in purgatory. The sacrament of penance, in conjunction with the penitential practices of the Church, can help us to attain complete purification from sin so that no punishment remains.

## Confession as a Meeting
## With the Forgiving Christ (C 1461–67)

When the Church forgives, Christ forgives. The priest is a sign of Christ's Real Presence in penance. We confess our sins to Christ, and Christ forgives us.

This means that the priest has a serious responsibility to show the same compassion and understanding Christ showed to sinners. Most priests realize this and act accordingly. However, priests are human; they can fail to show Christ's mercy to penitents, just as parents can fail to show Christ's love to their children. Penitents who encounter a priest seriously lacking in compassion or understanding should pray for that priest, but they should also seek out another confessor.

All priests are bound to observe the "seal of confession." They may not disclose what is told in confession and may not use it against a penitent in any way.

Some penitents are afraid that the priest might look down on them because of their sins. Such penitents should remember that any priest who did this would be committing a terrible sin of pride, worse than anything the penitent might have confessed to him. Further, confessors hear every sin imaginable, and nothing they are told will shock them. Most priests would agree with this statement of an experienced confessor: "When people confess sins that they think are especially shameful, I don't look down on them but respect them for their courage and honesty." Finally, penitents should remember that priests go to confession too!

## Overcoming Problems (C 1485–98)

We can learn many things by observing others, but we cannot learn about penance in this way. As a result, people who join the Church are sometimes uneasy about penance, even after it has been explained. Catholics who have been away from confession for many years may be uncertain about what to do or may fear that they will panic and forget everything. Such individuals need only mention to the priest that they are unsure or fearful and ask for his help.

At times we may confess our sins and afterward realize that we forgot something we had intended to tell. If this happens, we can simply mention it the next time we go to confession. A person may deliberately fail to confess a serious sin out of fear or shame, then carry a burden of worry and doubt, perhaps for many years. Such an individual can tell the priest, "Father, I was afraid to confess something a few years ago, and I need your help."

Some people are terribly damaged by their own sins or the sins of others. People who are weighed down by burdens of infidelity, abortion, child abuse, or other sins sometimes tell the priest: "I feel so guilty. I just don't see how Christ can forgive me." Such a person should meditate on the following: "Suppose someone came to you with exactly the same sins and feelings of guilt you now have. You would not treat that person harshly, would you? If you can be understanding and forgiving (because you know how that person feels!), will not Christ be at least as understanding and forgiving as you are? And will not Jesus, who forgave Peter for denying him and Paul for putting innocent Christians to death, forgive you too?"

Another problem is described by this complaint: "I use penance regularly, but I keep confessing the old sins. It doesn't seem to do me any good." People who feel this way may not realize that if they were not using penance they would be slipping back! Actually, they may be making progress but feel otherwise because they are becoming more sensitive to the sin in their lives.

When we become discouraged with our weaknesses and the frequency with which failings seem to rise up, we should realize that the soul is like a flower garden. The better the soil is, the more beautiful the flowers. But good soil means that weeds can grow too. We pull them out, and they grow back again! Pulling out weeds is a necessary part of gardening. So it is with our lives. The soul may be beautiful with the flowers of virtue, but the weeds of sin keep coming up. We "pull them out" in the sacrament of penance...over and over again. And we never forget: "A saint is a sinner who keeps trying!"

### *Questions for Discussion or Reflection*

When a penitent confesses serious sin, does Christ change his attitude toward that person? Does God love us less before confession? If God does not change when we confess, what does?

Some people criticize Catholics because "they go to confession and then commit the same sins again." Is there some truth in this accusation? Can our sins be forgiven if we fear we may commit the same sins again? If we intend to commit the same sins?

How often should Catholics go to confession? once a year? once a month? Why?

### *Activities*

Spend a few minutes thanking Jesus for penance. Ask the Holy Spirit to give you God's attitude toward this sacrament. Meditate on the Lord's Prayer: "Forgive us our trespasses as we forgive those who trespass against us." Reflect: When I am asked for forgiveness by others, do I show the kind of compassion and mercy I want from Jesus? (Matthew 18:21-35).

*You may wish to memorize the following prayer:*

### *Act of Contrition*

My God, I am sorry for my sins with all my heart. In choosing to do wrong and failing to do good, I have sinned against you whom I should love above all things. I firmly intend, with your help, to do penance, to sin no more, and to avoid whatever leads me to sin. Our Savior Jesus Christ suffered and died for us. In his name, my God, have mercy. Amen.

# CHAPTER ELEVEN
## The Anointing of the Sick— Jesus Heals

We look at the beauty of the earth and see the handiwork of God. We discover in our vast universe a plan that bears the seal of a divine architect. At such times, we feel secure and loved, and we easily believe that our hearts are made for God.

But when a tornado sweeps across the landscape leaving a trail of splintered buildings and shattered bodies, we may question why God allows such tragedy. When we step into the lobby of a children's hospital, we may wonder how this place fits into the divine plan. When we sit in doctors' offices dreading the word *malignant*, we may feel fear pushing faith from our hearts.

Tragedy, suffering, sickness, and death pose formidable obstacles to belief. There is so much pain. If there is a good God, why must this be? How can we trust that Jesus will heal when we cannot understand why God allows the pain?

### Why? (C 272–74, 309–24)

The temptation is to find an easy answer to the "why" of suffering. In Old Testament times, for example, people did not make distinctions between "causing" and "allowing." Since God is all-powerful, they believed that God had to be the cause of everything. If someone made a wicked choice, it was God who caused it. Thus, "the LORD made Pharaoh obstinate, and he would not let the Israelites leave his land" (Exodus 11:10). The Israelites did not understand natural laws, like the law of gravity: If someone leaped from a building and was killed, they felt that God caused the person's death. They believed also that if God caused something bad, God must have a good reason. Usually that reason was punishment for sin; so if people suffered, it was because they had sinned. The Book of Job was written to challenge these assumptions, as well as other "easy answers" of the time. Job concludes that human beings cannot understand the designs of God.

The contemporaries of Jesus were still confused about the causes of suffering, as is clear from the attitude of Jesus' followers when they saw a blind man. "His disciples asked him, 'Rabbi, who sinned, this man or his parents, that he was born blind?'" (John 9:2). Jesus answered that neither the blind man nor his parents had sinned but that his blindness was permitted "so that the works of God might be made visible through him" (John 9:3). In other words God did not cause the blindness. God was on the side of the blind man, ready to help through the healing hand of Jesus. God does not cause our suffering. God may *allow* it for reasons we do not understand, but God is on our side.

God gives us freedom so that we can freely love. God does not take freedom away when we choose the wrong thing or when we choose evil. God won't catch us if we fall from a ten-story window. God won't reach out to stop a bullet from a murderer's gun. God won't destroy a criminal to prevent evil. If God would do these things, all of us would be forced to make only good choices. We would be mere puppets, incapable of freedom and love.

We live in a world where for hundreds of thousands of years people have been making free choices, many of them bad. As a result the human race is far from what it should be. Instead of using our talents for the past half-million years to learn how to live in harmony with one another and with creation, we have created weapons for destruction and upset the balance of nature. We pass on problems and diseases in ways we may never understand. Long ago, for example, someone might have misused alcohol, introducing genetic mutations that endure for generations and cause cancer in a descendant. God is not punishing an individual today by sending cancer. Rather, it is a consequence of human freedom and natural laws as inevitable as hitting the ground after a fall. It just takes longer. God does not interfere with the natural process. God lets it happen because freedom is so essential to our being truly human, loving, and responsible. Yes, there have been some occasions in human history when God intervened to change the consequences of natural laws, but such interventions are "miraculous." If they were the normal course of events, they would require an entirely different universe, one with no freedom and no love. In a very real sense, God cannot eliminate all tragedies, accidents, and illness.

## God Is Love (C 302–08, 312)

But God does everything that is possible! "God is love" (1 John 4:16). God is always present to help us make the most of whatever happens. If we open ourselves to God's love, presence, and power, God will do what "love" can do.

Since we live in a world that is the result of God's love, when we freely turn to that love, great things can happen. This is true even in natural circumstances. Consider, for example, the case of two children who undergo major surgery. Afterward one is given medical treatment in isolation, while the other is given the same treatment, plus plenty of love and attention from staff, family, and friends. The second child, energized by love, will recover more quickly. So, too, when we are in touch with God, God's love can do great things for us, even bringing us better physical and emotional health.

Of course, love can't do everything. It can't stop a bullet or heal every illness or eradicate all the effects of old age. But love will help us make the most of every situation. Love will often make healing possible in circumstances that seem hopeless. Love will strengthen us to cope with disabilities and turn them into victories. Finally, love will do what really matters: it will strengthen us to cope with any illness, any accident, any loss, even death itself.

Miracles do happen, by God's power, and we can always hope and pray for them. But they are miracles precisely because they do not fit into any definite pattern. They are not the automatic result of praying with a certain degree of faith. The presence of a miracle does not mean that God loves one person more than another. The absence of a miracle does not show any lack of love on God's part. After all, Jesus suffered the agony of crucifixion and the horror of death on a cross after praying to his Father for deliverance.

The cross teaches us that there is no easy answer to the problem of pain. Jesus did not eliminate suffering, but immersed himself in it. When we are immersed in pain, our union with the suffering Christ can help us endure. Even when we feel abandoned, as Jesus did when he cried out, "My God, my God, why have you forsaken me?" (Matthew 27:46), Jesus can bring us to trust and peace: "Father, into your hands I commend my spirit" (Luke 23:46).

The cross can help us see that while suffering is not good in itself, it can lead to good. Few things in life involve more love and courage than the patient acceptance of suffering, especially when our suffering benefits others. A mother accepts the pains of birth to bring her child into the world. A father endures the fatigue of hard physical labor to support his family. A paraplegic ignores disabilities in order to be of service to others. Pain is not attractive, but the heroism and courage required to overcome pain are among the greatest values of human existence.

The suffering of Jesus on the cross can also help us realize that while God does not cause pain, God is present to us in our pain. When a child is badly injured by a drunken driver, this is not "God's will." But God is there, helping those involved to endure what must be suffered and to rise above it, to foster whatever healing is possible, to comfort the child's parents. God is present to us in every pain-filled hour as God was present to Jesus on the cross.

And just as the suffering of Jesus was redemptive, so our suffering, by God's grace, can be redemptive. Paul wrote, "Now I rejoice in my sufferings for your sake, and in my flesh I am filling up what is lacking in the afflictions of Christ on behalf of his body, which is the church" (Colossians 1:24). Christ's death was sufficient to redeem humankind, of course, but Christ needs us now if his love and grace are to be channeled to others. When we offer up our suffering on behalf of others, it becomes a powerful prayer calling down the love and mercy of God. Christ allows us to do more than endure suffering. He makes it possible for us to turn suffering into prayer.

We may not fully understand suffering, but it does not separate us from God's love and it can be conquered: "If God is for us, who can be against us?...What will separate us from the love of Christ? Will anguish, or distress, or persecution, or famine, or nakedness, or peril, or the sword?...No, in all these things we conquer overwhelmingly through him who loved us. For I am convinced that neither death, nor life...nor any other creature will be able to separate us from the love of God in Christ Jesus our Lord" (Romans 8:31,35-39).

## Healing in the Bible (C 1499–1505)

People of the Old Testament believed in the power of prayer and in the efficacy of medicine. Seven hundred years before Christ, King Hezekiah became critically ill. He prayed to God, who responded, "I will heal you." The prophet Isaiah then prescribed a poultice for the boil causing Hezekiah's illness. In three days Hezekiah was well (Isaiah 38). The Book of Sirach bids us: "Hold the physician in honor, for he is essential to you, and God it was who established his profession....When you are ill, delay not, but pray to God, who will heal you....Then give the doctor his place... for you need him too....And he too beseeches God that his diagnosis may be correct and his treatment bring about a cure" (38:1, 9, 12, 14).

Jesus worked many miracles of healing, sometimes by a word and sometimes by methods then regarded as medicinal. Mark records that Jesus used spittle to heal the deaf and the blind (7:31-37; 8:22-26). Spittle was thought by the ancients to have healing properties. (Even today we place a cut or burned finger into our mouths to ease the pain.) Jesus might have been quoting a proverb when he said, "Those who are well do not need a physician, but the sick do" (Matthew 9:12), but its truth was taken for granted by his listeners. One of the early preachers of the gospel was "Luke the beloved physician" (Colossians 4:14).

These passages show that the Bible sees no contradiction between prayer and medicine. The Catholic Church has always believed in the power of prayer and in the efficacy of good medical care. The Church has had a long tradition of building both churches and hospitals.

## Anointing of the Sick (C 1506–32)

Jesus once sent his Twelve Apostles two by two to teach and heal in his name: "So they went off and preached repentance. They drove out many demons, and they anointed with oil many who were sick and cured them" (Mark 6:12-13). Oil and oil-based medications were used for healing in the ancient world, and this is another example of a physical sign being used to mediate the power of God.

After the Resurrection of Jesus, an anointing with oil brought his healing to the sick: "Is anyone among you sick? He should summon the presbyters of the church, and they should pray over him and anoint [him] with oil in the name of the Lord, and the prayer of faith will save the sick person, and the Lord will raise him up. If he has committed any sins, he will be forgiven" (James 5:14-15).

This passage is seen by the Catholic Church as Christ's design for the sacrament of anointing of the sick. It shows that such an anointing was given by the early Church, that the minister was a Church leader (presbyter, priest), and that Christ was present through the anointing and prayer to bring healing. The exact kind of healing is not specified. The expressions "save" and "raise up" might refer to a physical cure, spiritual healing, or being raised to eternal life.

For eight hundred years healing was the chief purpose of the sacrament. Gradually, however, the anointing was associated primarily with critical illness and death, and by the twelfth century the sacrament was commonly seen as preparation for death and was called by such names as extreme unction (Last Anointing) and the sacrament of the dying. The Council of Trent countered this trend somewhat by pointing out that the sacrament had numerous spiritual and physical effects, including health of body when this would promote spiritual welfare. But until the Second Vatican Council, the emphasis of anointing continued to be preparation for death. This Council stated that the sacrament should be called the anointing of the sick and taught that it is not reserved for those at the point of death, but is meant to bring healing and salvation to the seriously ill.

The pastoral practice of the Church today calls for the anointing of the sick in case of serious illness—physical, emotional, or mental. Thus a person might be anointed when sick with pneumonia, when preparing for surgery, when seriously depressed, or when weak from the burdens of old age. Anointing would not usually be ministered for colds or other minor illnesses. The sacrament may be repeated in case of long-term illness, especially when there is a change for the worse. Anointing of the sick may be ministered in a continuous rite with penance and holy Communion. When a person is dying, these three sacraments may properly be called the last rites. When holy Communion is given to a dying person, it is called *viaticum*—"[Christ] on the way with you."

There is a communal rite of anointing which may be celebrated as a healing service for the seriously ill in nursing homes, hospices, hospitals, and parishes. Anointing may also be given during the celebration of Mass.

Scripture readings and prayers for healing accompany the anointing. All baptized believers who are present join with the priest in asking for God's grace. The priest, after laying hands on the head of the sick person, anoints the forehead with blessed oil as he prays: "Through this holy anointing may the Lord in his love and mercy help you with the grace of the Holy Spirit." He anoints the hands, saying, "May the Lord who frees you from sin save you and raise you up."

The ritual for the sacrament of anointing explains that this sacrament gives God's grace to the sick for the good of the whole person. The sick are encouraged to trust in God and are fortified against temptations and anxiety. They are helped to bear suffering bravely and to conquer it. They are strengthened by God for a return to physical health if this will be beneficial to their salvation, or for their entry into everlasting life. If they are unable to receive the sacrament of penance, their sins are forgiven by the anointing.

### How to Pray for the Sick (C 1508)

The Catholic Church acknowledges that prayers for the sick may be answered in many ways by God. Sometimes anointing results in cures that seem miraculous. Sometimes the healing process is hastened by anointing. Sometimes there appears to be little physical improvement, but the sick person is enabled to bear suffering patiently. Sometimes the person is given peace and hope in the face of approaching death. With so many possible outcomes, how do we know what to pray for when we or others are sick?

First of all, we should realize that we do not pray as if God had to be convinced to desire what is best for the sick! God always desires what is best, and we pray in order to place the sick in the healing presence of God. Prayer removes the obstacles between us and God, obstacles like sin, materialism, fear, and depression. Prayer opens us up to God's love and to God's gifts of healing or of eternal life.

Second, we must pray as Jesus did in the Garden of Gethsemane: "My Father, if it is possible, let this cup pass from me; yet, not as I will, but as you will" (Matthew 26:39). We simply do not know how our suffering fits into God's plan, and while we may always pray for healing, it must be with openness to the will of God. In this we are helped by the Holy Spirit: "The Spirit too comes to the aid of our weakness; for we do not know how to pray as we ought, but the Spirit itself intercedes with inexpressible groanings" (Romans 8:26).

Third, we should become aware of the astounding possibilities for healing which God has built into our bodies, minds, and emotions, and into our relationships with others. Modern medical research has uncovered incredible agents for healing in our blood and bodily organs. They are most effective when our minds are thinking positively and our emotions are optimistic. Prayer brings body, mind, and emotions together for the battle against illness. Much study is being given to "right-brain" and "left-brain" activity, and researchers are learning that we have God-given powers that we have only begun to tap. Such powers pour reserves of strength into our bodies in crises, as when a mother lifts a car off the injured body of her child after an accident. Such powers allow people to affect others over great distances, as when one identical twin "senses" that the other is undergoing a traumatic experience. There are some researchers who claim that when people pray for the recovery of an individual, the prayer has effects that are measurable. It may be that prayer opens us up to healing gifts which God has given us but which have lain hidden, gifts which God wants us to discover and use.

Fourth, we should be wary of the claim, "If you pray with enough faith, you will always be healed." It just isn't so. Paul reports that he suffered from a "thorn in the flesh" and begged the Lord that it might leave him. God's response was, "My grace is sufficient for you, for power is made perfect in weakness" (2 Corinthians 12:7-9). God did not remove Paul's suffering but gave him strength to bear it. Paul is presented in the New Testament as acknowledging the persistent nature of some illnesses. In 1 Timothy 5:23, Paul writes, "Stop drinking only water, but have a little wine for the sake of your stomach and your frequent illnesses." In 2 Timothy 4:20, Paul relates, "I left Trophimus sick at Miletus." If sickness always yielded to prayers of sufficient faith, Paul's prayer would have healed Timothy and Trophimus.

Fifth, we need to realize that we all must die. Every person miraculously healed by Jesus died eventually from sickness, injury, or old age. Death is the only complete healing. Death frees us from a body vulnerable to disease, injuries, and the ravages of age. In death our physical body is transformed into a spiritual body, and we are brought to the fullness of life and vitality, where there will be "no more death or mourning, wailing or pain" (Revelation 21:4).

How do we pray? We pray with confidence in God's love for us. We pray to the Father, "Thy will be done." We pray in the hope of opening ourselves, the sick, and those caring for the sick to the graciousness and guidance of God and to whatever healing is possible. We pray free from nagging doubts that healing might come "if we just had more faith." We pray with the peaceful realization that when sickness seems to close a door in death, Christ opens that door to eternal life.

### Words, Images, and Gestures (C 1509)

One way to pray for healing for ourselves or others is simply to talk to God in our own words. We speak to God about the pain, tell God we want to pray in union with Jesus, and ask for openness to all the healing God can give. If a friend is in surgery, we ask God to grant healing and to guide the doctors and nurses. We ask God to remove any hindrances to healing. We thank God for the loving care always available to us.

Another way to pray is with images. If we are sick, we may picture Christ standing at our bedside, placing his hands on us as he did on the sick in the gospels. We picture our disabilities flowing from us, as the strength and healing of Jesus fill our body, mind, and heart. We can pray like this for others, and we may also visualize Christ standing at the side of doctors and nurses as they care for the sick.

When we visit the sick, we should ask if they would like us to pray with them or for them. They may wish to join us in the Lord's Prayer or in other prayers. They might appreciate our reading short Bible passages pertaining to healing. It might be appropriate to hold the hand of the sick person as we pray. We should be sensitive to the needs of the sick, but we ought not refrain from prayer just because we are shy or fearful.

Prayer can be a great source of healing in families. When a parent places a bandage on a child's injury, a little prayer like "May Jesus bless you and make you feel better" brings Christ into the healing process. If a small child is sick, other members of the family can gather around, place hands on the child, and ask God for healing. They should remind the child that Jesus is also present, letting his love and healing power flow into the child.

Today many parishes have "prayer lines." When someone is seriously sick or injured, members of the prayer line inform one another by phone and then pray for the person. Often the sick report that they feel lifted up and strengthened by the prayer of so many.

Only God knows how much healing is available in answer to sincere prayer. If believers could see themselves as members of the Body of Christ, the divine Physician, and pray accordingly, wonderful gifts of healing could result.

## Comforting the Sorrowful (C 1680–90, 2447–49)

One of the most important opportunities we have of transmitting Christ's healing power is in comforting those who grieve. Grief comes to those who suffer a serious loss. It is a natural process, but it can be as debilitating as sickness.

When we reach out to others in their grief, we bring them the healing of Christ. In this, as in all things, Christ is our model. We see Jesus, for example, comforting his friends Martha and Mary at the death of their brother Lazarus, and then—as the "resurrection and the life"—bringing Lazarus back to life (John 11). We can't bring the dead back to life as Christ did, but we can bring sympathy and hope to those weighed down by grief.

Grief touches many people: relatives of someone who has died, a couple experiencing a miscarriage, a friend undergoing surgery, a childless couple, people going through a divorce, a family losing their farm or business, an acquaintance who has had to place a parent in a nursing home.

In order to help such people, we should realize that those who grieve may go through five stages: *denial*—"This can't be happening to me"; *anger*—against God, others, one's self; *bargaining*—"God, if you'll change this, I'll do anything you want"; *depression*—sadness, weariness, wanting to give up; *acceptance*—"This is a part of life, and I must go on from here." These stages may come and go, not necessarily in the order given. People may find themselves in and out of them for years. Anniversaries and holidays are especially hard times when painful feelings recur.

What should we do or say when a friend or relative suffers

loss? The first thing is presence, just being available—a visit, a card, a gift. Second, we can express our sympathy in simple and honest ways: "I'm sorry about....I'm praying for you." Third, if people want to discuss their feelings, it is crucial that we listen and accept them. If they express denial, anger, bargaining, or depression, we don't have to try to talk them out of it. If they are allowed to go through the process, they'll reach acceptance sooner. Someone, for example, may be saying over and over, "I can't believe this is happening to me; God is unjust" (denial and anger). Our tendency might be to respond, "Well, it is happening, and you mustn't say things like that about God!" It would be much better just to listen and to say gently, "I'm so sorry you have to go through this pain."

The Church comforts the sorrowful through its funeral rites. Prayer vigils at the funeral home, the funeral liturgy, and the final commendation and committal ceremonies acknowledge the grief of the bereaved and affirm Christ's promise of eternal life. Jesus seems to be present in a special way at these rites to comfort the sorrowful and to help his people place their loved ones in God's merciful care. Jesus touches the bereaved through the prayers and liturgy of the Church and through the presence and love of its members.

Jesus was sensitive to the grief of Martha and Mary (see John 11:21-45). He wasn't afraid to cry. He was there for them and met their needs. Even before he raised Lazarus, he brought consolation and hope. We can bring comfort to others because we are followers of Jesus. We can bring hope because we believe in eternal life. Above all, we can bring Jesus himself, for the Spirit of God dwells in us, and Christ lives in us (Romans 8:10-11). Through us, Christ comforts those who mourn.

### Again, Why? (C 1526–32)

Tragedy, suffering, sickness, and death are indeed formidable obstacles to belief. But when we see them as consequences of human freedom, when we remember that Jesus himself faced up to them, when we believe that God is near us through anointing and the prayer of the Church, when we are supported by other members of the Body of Christ, these obstacles can be overcome. Then we can say with Paul, "I consider that the sufferings of this present time are as nothing compared with the glory to be revealed for us" (Romans 8:18).

## Questions for Discussion or Reflection

Have you ever heard the questions, "Can God make a square circle?" "Can God make a rock so big that God can't pick it up?" Do these questions mean that there are things God cannot do? Can God make a world where people are free and then remove all the unpleasant consequences of freedom?

A woman was standing beside the casket of her daughter who had been killed in an automobile accident. A well-meaning friend came up to her and said, "It was God's will." Was it?

These are comments made to people experiencing grief: "Don't cry; it'll be all right." "You'll get over it." "You don't know how lucky you are." "You should be over it by now." "I know just how you feel." "At least you had each other for years." "You're still young and you have plenty of time to have another child." "Time heals all." "God sends such crosses only to real believers." "It's all for the best." "It's God's will." "There's a reason for this." Evaluate these comments. Do you think they bring comfort to the sorrowing? What can we say to the grieving that will be helpful?

What has Jesus done to prove that God is on your side when you are suffering? What more could Jesus do? What do you think of the statement, "Death is the only complete healing"?

## Activities

Tonight, before you fall asleep, form a mental image of Jesus coming to your bedside. Picture him placing his hands on your head to comfort and heal you. Ask him to deliver you from any physical illness or pain that may be troubling you. Ask him to replace any harmful feelings such as fear, depression, resentment, anxiety, and hatred with his grace and love. Ask Jesus to fill your heart and your whole being with the blessings of the Holy Spirit mentioned by Paul in Galatians 5:22: love, joy, peace, patience, kindness, generosity, faith, gentleness, and self-control, qualities which will make you open to the healing presence of God.

You may use the same prayer in reference to others. Picture Jesus standing at their bedsides, giving them his healing and peace.

# CHAPTER TWELVE
## The Priesthood—Jesus Ministers

A prisoner had escaped from Auschwitz. In retaliation, the Nazi commandant summoned the other prisoners and chose ten to be starved to death. One of them sobbed, "My wife, my children!" A forty-seven-year-old Catholic priest, Father Maximilian Kolbe, stepped forward. "I want to die in place of this prisoner," he said. The commandant hesitated, then snapped, "Request granted."

Bishop Fulton Sheen looked into the camera and into the eyes of the largest television audience of his day. He ended his explanation of Catholic doctrine with a smile and the words, "God love you."

Tens of thousands of people stood in Yankee Stadium. Pope John Paul II began Mass, "In the name of the Father, and of the Son, and of the Holy Spirit."

These are twentieth-century images of the priesthood.

A businessman paused at his desk. He was struggling with a decision that would affect all his employees. He picked up his Bible, read from it, and prayed.

The young family hurried into a pew. They knelt for a few moments, then rose with the congregation to sing the opening hymn—but only after the mother separated the two smallest children who had been busily elbowing each other.

A schoolteacher, tired after a long day with twenty squirming first graders, stood on "bus duty." She chatted with the children, tossed a ball back and forth with a shy little girl, and answered questions about a homework assignment.

These, too, are twentieth-century images of the priesthood.

## The Ordained Priesthood and the Priesthood of the Faithful (C 783–86, 871–79, 897–913, 1533–35)

Most Catholics could easily identify Father Kolbe, Bishop Sheen, and Pope John Paul II as priests. They might not recognize the businessman, family, and teacher as priests. But they are, according to God's Word in the Bible and the Church's teaching.

The word *priest* comes from the Greek *presbyteros*, meaning "elder," and refers to someone authorized to perform the sacred rites of a religion, someone who is a mediator or link between God and people. In the Old Testament priests came from families tracing their lineage to Aaron or Levi. As consecrated ministers they held a special place of leadership in worship. But there was also a "priesthood of the people." God said to the Jews, "You shall be to me a kingdom of priests, a holy nation" (Exodus 19:6). All the people were dedicated to God and participated in the sacrifices offered by the consecrated priests.

The New Testament Church laid the foundation of an ordained priesthood. But it also recognized a priesthood of the faithful: "You are 'a chosen race, a royal priesthood, a holy nation, a people of his own, so that you may announce the praises' of him who called you out of darkness into his wonderful light" (1 Peter 2:9).

The Second Vatican Council in its document the *Dogmatic Constitution on the Church* taught that the baptized are consecrated as the "common priesthood of the faithful." This differs from the ordained priesthood, but is a real participation in Christ's priesthood. According to the Council, the faithful exercise their priesthood by joining in the offering of Mass and sacraments, by prayer, and by the witness of a holy life.

This has important implications for all Catholics. It means that they come to Mass not as mere spectators, but as people who offer their lives with Christ to God. All Catholics have a priestly offering, their own particular circumstances of life, which no one else can present (Romans 12:1). Catholics can also be active participants in the celebration of other sacraments in union with Christ.

The priesthood of the faithful means also that our prayers are part of the priestly prayer of Christ. Whether we pray individually or with others, we make our prayer with Jesus. This reality encourages us to pray with faith and confidence. Jesus Christ, our

High Priest, is always at our side. "Therefore, since we have a great high priest who has passed through the heavens, Jesus, the Son of God, let us hold fast to our confession....Let us confidently approach the throne of grace to receive mercy and to find grace for timely help" (Hebrews 4:14-16).

The priesthood of the faithful means that Christ depends upon us to carry on his priestly mission by the witness of our lives. Christ offered himself as his priestly sacrifice (Hebrews 7:27). All our thoughts, words, and actions can become a part of the offering of Christ and give witness to the loving action of God in our world. The traditional Catholic practice of the morning offering, by which we offer to God our day, is a beautiful expression of this fact. "Through him [Christ] then let us continually offer God a sacrifice of praise, that is, the fruit of lips that confess his name. Do not neglect to do good and to share what you have; God is pleased by sacrifices of that kind" (Hebrews 13:15-16).

### The Single Vocation (C 900, 1658)

The context of the priesthood of the faithful is an appropriate place to point out the importance of the single vocation. Many individuals are called to follow Christ as single Catholics, and this vocation offers abundant opportunities to do great things for God.

By baptism and confirmation single Catholics are united to Christ and commissioned to continue his mission. They are to be Christ in the workplace and other arenas of daily life. By participating in the Mass and sacraments, by prayer, and by the witness of their lives, single Catholics bring Christ to the world.

Being single gives many Catholics the opportunity to pursue specialized fields of service. Doctors, nurses, teachers, and others can choose to be single in order to help others. Their vocations allow them to bring Christ into situations that might not be reached as effectively by priests, religious, or married couples.

Singles should realize that their first ministry is their daily lives. They serve Christ by going to work, participating in government and civic affairs, interacting with family and friends, and enjoying recreational and social activities. Many singles are also active in church ministries: they teach religion, sing in choirs, read Scripture at Mass, help as eucharistic ministers, and serve on parish councils and other parish organizations.

The single vocation is a call to be part of the priesthood of the faithful, to continue the work of Christ, who served his Father as a single person in the world.

## The Ordained Priesthood (C 1536–54)

Old Testament traditions place the origins of the priesthood with the tribe of Levi (Deuteronomy 33:8-11) and with the family of Aaron (Exodus 28-29). Priests led the people in worship, interpreted God's will, and taught the law of God. After the exiles returned from Babylon, the office of high priest developed into the most important position in Israel. The high priest was the head of Israelite worship, president of the Sanhedrin (the main Jewish tribunal), and chief representative of the people to the various foreign powers that ruled Israel.

The followers of Jesus at first worshiped in the Temple after his Resurrection and met in their own homes for the "breaking of the bread." When Jewish leaders began persecuting the Church, Christians developed their own structure and positions of leadership, based on what Jesus had taught and done. The New Testament mentions the Twelve Apostles as having special prominence. There were also other apostles (like Paul), prophets, teachers, miracle workers, healers, helpers, administrators, interpreters (1 Corinthians 12:28), evangelists, pastors (Ephesians 4:11), deacons (Acts 6:1-6), presbyters (1 Timothy 5:17-22), and bishops (1 Timothy 3:1-7; Titus 1:5-9). In the New Testament there is no clear explanation of the interrelationship among these offices, and their functions probably varied in different locations.

But there is evidence from other sources that the offices of bishop, priest, and deacon began very early to take on the characteristics we see in them today. (The sacrament of holy orders is so named from the three offices, or "orders," of bishop, priest, and deacon.) Ignatius of Antioch, who died in A.D. 108, wrote letters to local churches presided over by a bishop; he provides evidence that bishops and priests celebrated the Eucharist. Hippolytus of Rome, who died in A.D. 236, describes how the bishop ordained other bishops, priests, and deacons by the imposition of hands. This pattern of ordination is essential to the Catholic Church, which traces a line of succession from the apostles to the bishops of the present day.

As the Church grew, bishops became leaders of geographical areas called dioceses; they were assisted by priests and deacons.

There have been times when Church leaders exercised considerable power over temporal governments and times when political rulers controlled ecclesiastical leaders. Generally, when the roles of church and state became intertwined, the Church suffered, either because it was oppressed or because it became too involved in temporal matters. In the past one hundred years the Church has moved away from political entanglements. As the result, its influence in spiritual matters has been strengthened, and Church leaders have grown in credibility and influence.

### Deacons (C 1569–71, 1588)

In the Acts of the Apostles we read that deacons were first ordained by the apostles to care for the poor (Acts 6:1-7). (The Greek word *diakonia* means helper.) They soon began to carry out other ministries. Stephen preached the gospel and was martyred for witnessing to Jesus (Acts 6–7). Philip preached in Samaria and elsewhere, instructing people and baptizing (Acts 8).

Eventually, the role of deacon disappeared except as a final step to the priesthood, but was revived as a ministry after Vatican II. Deacons, both married and single, assist the priest at the altar during Mass, read the gospel, preach, baptize, witness marriages, conduct funerals, and perform many other functions important to the life of the Church.

### Priests (C 1562–68, 1572–85, 1587)

"You are a priest forever, according to the order of Melchizedek" (Psalm 110:4). These words from the Old Testament were understood by early Christians as prophetic of the priesthood of Jesus Christ. The lineage of Jesus did not go back to Levi or Aaron, and the author of the Letter to the Hebrews saw in Psalm 110 an indication of God's intent to replace the Israelite priesthood with a new one. Melchizedek was a king and "priest of God most high." He offered bread and wine to the Lord in the presence of Abraham, who gave him tithes, thus acknowledging his superiority. Therefore, the priesthood of Christ is superior to that of Levi and Aaron, descendants of Abraham (Hebrews 5–7; Genesis 14:18-20).

The Catholic Church, guided by the Holy Spirit, saw the Eucharist as an offering of bread and wine, which became the body and blood of the great King and Priest, Jesus Christ. It has been the function of priests to continue this sacrificial mission of Jesus and to continue as well his prophetic mission of teaching and his kingly mission of leading.

Priests continue the **priestly** ministry of Christ. They celebrate the sacraments and lead others in worship. Their greatest privilege is to pray the words of Christ over the bread and wine: "This is my body. This is the cup of my blood." Priests baptize, confirm (when welcoming adults into the Church), hear confessions, witness marriages, anoint the sick, and bury the dead. They pray the Liturgy of the Hours, the daily prayer of the Church.

Priests continue the **prophetic** ministry of Christ by preaching, by teaching religion classes in elementary schools, high schools, and universities, and by explaining the faith to converts. They counsel individuals and families.

Priests continue the **kingly** ministry of Christ by serving as administrators. They work with parish councils and other organizations to keep parish life functioning effectively. They may be involved in works of charity, social justice, and ecumenism (unity among churches). They cooperate with other priests at neighboring parishes and with diocesan leaders to coordinate the work of the Church in their diocese.

Priests must witness to Christ by the manner of their lives. A well-known aspect of priestly witness is celibacy, the voluntary state of not marrying and of abstaining from sexual intercourse. The roots of celibacy are found in the New Testament. Christ himself was celibate. He spoke of those who "have renounced marriage for the sake of the kingdom of heaven" (Matthew 19:12). Paul praised celibacy as a means of focusing on "the things of the Lord" (1 Corinthians 7:32-34). Some priests in the early Church freely embraced celibacy, and eventually laws required celibacy of priests in various places. In A.D. 1139 the Second Lateran Council made celibacy mandatory for priests of the Latin Rite of the Roman Catholic Church. Married men may be ordained priests in Eastern Rite Catholic Churches, and today married ministers of other faiths who join the Roman Catholic Church and are ordained to the priesthood may remain married.

Recent popes have praised celibacy as a great gift of God to the Catholic Church, and it is surely that. Celibacy offers a unique opportunity to imitate the celibate Jesus. Celibacy frees priests from many concerns, as Paul suggests, to devote themselves to "the things of the Lord." Celibacy is a positive surrender of self to Christ, not just a negative renunciation, just as marriage is the positive choosing of one spouse, not just the renunciation of all others. Celibacy is a constant reminder to the priest that Jesus Christ is his first love and his source of strength. Celibacy creates a need that can be filled only by Jesus: It "demands" a strong prayer life between the priest and Jesus, just as marriage "demands" communication between husband and wife.

Celibacy also frees a priest to relate to many families, and it is one of the ways Jesus fulfills his promise: "Amen, I say to you, there is no one who has given up house or brothers or sisters or mother or father or children or lands for my sake and for the sake of the gospel who will not receive a hundred times more now in this present age: houses and brothers and sisters and mothers and children and lands, with persecutions, and eternal life in the age to come" (Mark 10:29-30).

Priests are usually addressed as "Father." This title suggests the family relationship a priest should have with members of the Church, as well as the attitudes of sacrifice and generosity with which a priest should serve his people. Thus, Paul said to the Corinthians: "I became your father in Christ Jesus through the gospel" (1 Corinthians 4:15). Some people criticize Catholics for calling priests "Father," stating that Jesus forbade this when he said, "Call no one on earth your father" (Matthew 23:9). But from the context it is clear that Jesus was speaking against false attitudes of pride and superiority. If this passage should be taken in a slavishly literal sense, then "father" could not be used in reference to parents!

Another term sometimes used of priests is *monsignor*. This is an honorary title conferred by bishops on priests because of important positions they may hold or because of special service to the Church.

In all that priests must be and do, they follow in the footsteps of Christ, the Good Shepherd. They have the responsibility and privilege of bringing the compassion, kindness, and generosity of Christ to the world. Being human, priests can fail, just as married couples can fail to show the love of Christ to their families and to the world. Some years ago priests were often "placed on a pedestal," as if their vocation alone raised them to a special level of sanctity. It wasn't so then and isn't so now. Priests have the same weaknesses as other human beings and struggle with the same temptations. They depend upon the grace of Christ just as others do. They need the support, love, and prayers of friends to keep them going.

### Bishops (C 883–896, 1555–61, 1586)

Bishops are leaders of church communities called dioceses, which vary in size and in number of parishes (local churches) and members. The word *bishop* comes from the Greek *episkopos*, meaning "overseer." Bishops are the successors of the apostles, and have the fullness of the priesthood. By A.D. 100, bishops were overseeing local churches. When problems arose, bishops met in councils to teach and guide church members over wider areas. Today all the bishops of the world in union with the pope are called the College of Bishops and as such are responsible not only for their own dioceses but also for the worldwide Church.

Originally, local bishops were elected by the people. Now the pope selects bishops, in consultation with the bishops and perhaps the priests of a given area. Bishops are ordained by other bishops, and in certain cases they may be ordained by the pope himself. In either event they are spiritual leaders in their dioceses, not just representatives of the pope.

Bishops carry out many of the same duties as priests but on a diocesan scale. Bishops ordain priests by the laying on of hands and invocation of the Holy Spirit. The bishop is a leader for the priests in his diocese, their "shepherd," and priests are in turn responsible to their bishop. Bishops have direct pastoral contact with laypersons when they travel to parishes for confirmation ceremonies and special events like church dedications. The church of the bishop is called a cathedral, and his office the chancery. The chancery is staffed by priests, nuns, and laypersons who are responsible for the administration of such diocesanwide ministries as worship, education, social justice, media, marriage preparation, annulments, finances, youth, and Catholic organizations.

Bishops also fulfill responsibilities to the Catholic Church at large by cooperating with other bishops at regional, national, and international levels. On the regional level dioceses are grouped together around an archdiocese, which is presided over by an archbishop. Regional groupings of bishops might meet to set common guidelines for marriage preparation, discuss problems in the area, or cooperate in charitable endeavors. The archbishop might preside over such meetings, but he does not have authority over the bishops in their own dioceses. On the national level in the United States, bishops belong to the National Council of Catholic Bishops and meet regularly to discuss national issues and determine policies. Documents issued by the NCCB, such as their statement on atomic weapons, can have considerable influence. Bishops are also called to work together for the good of the Church throughout the world. Occasionally, they all meet at ecumenical (general) councils to work with the pope on important issues. The most recent ecumenical council was the Second Vatican Council, held at Rome in 1962 to 1965.

Some bishops and archbishops are named cardinals by the pope. These are leaders who are in charge of important dioceses or who have high administrative positions in the Church. There are about one hundred cardinals from all over the world. They meet in Rome after the death of a pope to elect a new one.

## The Pope—Our Holy Father (C 551–53, 880–82, 888–92)

The United States has a president. College football teams choose captains. Civic groups elect chairpersons. Societies and organizations of every kind have leaders who are a sign of unity and purpose for each group. So it should not be surprising that the Catholic Church has a leader who is a sign of unity and purpose for its members. We call our leader the pope, a word which can be traced back to the Latin *papa* and the Greek *pappas*, both of which mean "father."

The Catholic Church believes that the papacy finds its origin in the mind of Christ and in the New Testament Church. One day Jesus asked the apostles, "Who do people say that the Son of Man is?" When they responded with John the Baptizer, Elijah, Jeremiah, or one of the prophets, Jesus asked, "But who do you say that I am?" Simon Peter replied, "You are the Messiah, the Son of the living God." Jesus was pleased with this answer, acknowledging that it had been inspired by God and that it indicated a special role for Peter: "Blessed are you, Simon son of Jonah. For flesh and blood has not revealed this to you, but my heavenly Father. And so I say to you, you are Peter, and upon this rock I will build my church, and the gates of the netherworld shall not prevail against it. I will give you the keys to the kingdom of heaven. Whatever you bind on earth shall be bound in heaven; and whatever you loose on earth shall be loosed in heaven" (Matthew 16:13-19).

The Catholic Church understands this passage as mandating a special place of leadership and authority for Peter. Many other New Testament passages reinforce this view. Peter is named first in the lists of the apostles (Mark 3:16-19); he is the central figure in gospel events such as the Transfiguration (Matthew 17:1-8). Even after denying Jesus, Peter is singled out by the Lord to shepherd the flock (John 21:15-19). In the Acts of the Apostles, Peter is the first to proclaim the gospel publicly and is the chief spokesman for the apostles (Acts 2:14-40).

Peter went to Rome where he was martyred. His successors as bishop of Rome were recognized as leaders among the bishops, just as Peter was recognized as leader among the apostles. Popes have been visible signs of Jesus' presence and action in the world and signs of unity for the Catholic Church, calling all to be one flock under one Shepherd.

There have been about two hundred sixty-five popes. Most have been good men and effective leaders. Many have been saints. Some have been sinners and have failed miserably in their roles as spiritual leaders. Such failures should not surprise us. Jesus chose twelve apostles, and Judas turned out to be a traitor. Peter denied him.

Even though popes can fail, Catholics believe that Christ will not allow the Church to be misled in essential matters of faith and morals. Thus the basis for our doctrine of papal "infallibility," which applies only when certain conditions are met: (1) the pope is speaking *ex cathedra*—that is, as leader of the whole Church; (2) he is dealing with faith or morals; (3) he is expressly defining the doctrine as a matter of faith. This has happened only once in the last one hundred years, when Pope Pius XII defined the doctrine of the Assumption in 1950.

Catholics believe that truths can be infallibly expressed when they are believed by the universal Church or taught by the College of Bishops in union with the pope. When the doctrine of the Assumption was defined, it had been the object of belief by Catholics from time immemorial, and most of the world's bishops recommended that it be defined as Catholic doctrine.

Solemnly defined doctrines of the Catholic Church are called dogmas. These are beliefs that must be accepted by all who wish to be members of the Church. They include such truths as the Holy Trinity, the Incarnation, Christ's divinity, the Real Presence of Jesus in the Eucharist, Mary's Immaculate Conception, her Assumption, and the beliefs we profess in the Nicene Creed and Apostles' Creed.

The Catholic Church, then, has a basic core of beliefs that are essential, but there are many areas of belief which allow for varied opinions. For example, the Catholic Church holds as dogma that the Bible is inspired by God, but the Church has defined very few specific interpretations of biblical passages. Most of what the pope presents in sermons and writings is not infallible teaching. However, Catholics should attend to the pope's noninfallible teaching, since it is an important way Christ guides his Church through the Holy Spirit.

The doctrine of infallibility can be seen as a great blessing for the Church. It gives us assurance that God will not allow the powers of the "netherworld" to lead the Church astray. It helps believers distinguish what is essential from what is not. A clear understanding of infallibility and its limits may also be seen as a safeguard against the misuse of authority. Where there is no doctrine of infallibility, those in authority can easily assume the aura of infallibility. Some who criticize the Catholic Church because of its doctrine of infallibility will insist that their interpretation of the Bible is the only correct one and that only their church members can be saved. Where there is no doctrine of infallibility, there is the temptation for leaders to claim infallibility in everything!

The popes of the twentieth century have become spiritual leaders to the world. Through modern means of communication and transportation, they have preached the gospel of Christ to "all nations" (Matthew 28:19). The papacy is not just an institution but Christ's gift to his Church. The successor of Peter is not just the pope but our Holy Father: priest, teacher, leader, and sign of unity.

## Religious Communities (C 914–33, 1618–20)

For much of the Catholic Church's history, religious communities have played an important role in keeping the spirit of Jesus Christ alive in the world. Religious communities are organizations of men and women who take vows of poverty, chastity, and obedience in order to follow Christ more faithfully. They include laypersons, deacons, priests, and bishops in their numbers. There are hundreds of religious communities in the Church, some numbering thousands of members worldwide and some embracing only a few members in a particular location.

By their vow of poverty, religious give up some control over material possessions. By chastity they pledge not to marry and so free themselves for the service of Christ. By obedience they agree to serve the larger needs of their community and of the Church. Some communities may take other vows, too, such as service to the poor. Religious communities of men may be made up of priests and Brothers, who take vows but are not ordained. Some communities of men or of women may dedicate themselves to prayer and remain inside monastery or convent walls. Others devote themselves to various kinds of ministries, living where they work. Whereas "diocesan" or "secular" priests are ordained for a certain diocese and usually remain there all their lives, religious may go where they are needed and may serve many different dioceses. Laypersons may be affiliated with religious communities as members of a Third Order, and there are also lay institutes that promote prayer and good works.

Generally, religious communities developed in response to the needs of the Church and to the leadership of a "founder." Thus the Jesuits, the largest Catholic community of men, were founded by Saint Ignatius of Loyola in 1534 to face the challenges of the era after Protestants separated from the Church. They are well known today for pastoral, educational, and missionary work. The Daughters of Charity, the largest community of women, were founded by Saint Vincent de Paul and Saint Louise de Marillac in 1633 to serve the poor in schools, hospitals, and orphanages. Some religious communities, like the Benedictines, have been in existence for more than fifteen hundred years. Others, like the Missionaries of Charity, founded by Mother Teresa of Calcutta in 1950, have had a great impact on the Church in a relatively short time.

### "A Holy Nation, A People of His Own" (C 934–45, 1589–1600)

"You are 'a chosen race, a royal priesthood, a holy nation, a people of his own, so that you may announce the praises' of him who called you out of darkness into his wonderful light" (1 Peter 2:9). This passage can help us see "priesthood" as a vocation of all believers. Hopefully, it will lead us to see ourselves—single, married, vowed, or ordained—as a family, a "people of God's own" who announce the praises of Christ and spread the Good News.

Hopefully, too, this vision of the priesthood of the faithful might help all Catholics see ordained ministers and vowed religious as brothers and sisters and pray for religious and priestly vocations. That would surely be in accordance with the heart of Jesus who said, "The harvest is abundant but the laborers are few; so ask the master of the harvest to send out laborers for his harvest" (Luke 10:2).

### *Questions for Discussion or Reflection*

Have you thought of yourself as sharing in the priesthood of Christ? What do you have to offer at Mass that no one else can? Do you pray for priests and religious, your bishop, the Holy Father? If a member of your immediate family expressed a desire to become a priest, Brother, or Sister, how would you react? Do you regularly ask God to "send laborers for the harvest"?

### *Activities*

Next time you attend Mass, pray for the priest. If he preaches well, thank God for this. If not, ask God to inspire the priest and to help you get at least one special blessing from each homily.

# CHAPTER THIRTEEN
## Marriage—Christ Shares God's Love With Us

S he lay quietly on her bed, staring out the window. Occasionally a moan escaped her lips, twisted downward at the corners by the same stroke which had immobilized her years before. Her husband entered the room, smiled, kissed her gently on the cheek, and repeated the words he'd spoken to her for sixty years, "Honey, you look beautiful. I love you." Ever so slowly, the expression on her face softened into a look of contentment and peace.

"Husbands, love your wives, even as Christ loved the church.... So [also] husbands should love their wives as their own bodies. He who loves his wife loves himself. For no one hates his own flesh but rather nourishes and cherishes it, even as Christ does the church, because we are members of his body. 'For this reason a man shall leave [his] father and [his] mother and be joined to his wife, and the two shall become one flesh.' This is a great mystery, but I speak in reference to Christ and the church" (Ephesians 5:25-32).

In this passage Paul sees marriage as a sign, a sacrament, showing how Christ loves the Church. For almost two thousand years Christian married couples have shown the world that "God is love" (1 John 4:16), that Christ loves the Church (John 13:1), and that the greatest gift of the Holy Spirit is love (1 Corinthians 13).

When we witness an old man kissing his wife with gentleness and love, we stand in the presence of the sacred. We are touched by the realization that such love elevates human life to its most solemn beauty. We picture the couple sixty years ago, young newlyweds with hopes and dreams for the future. We see them raising their children, sharing hard work and hard times. We walk with them through middle age to where they are today. We visualize friendships and partings, fun and failure, health and sickness, prayer and pain, days and weeks and months and years of all the building blocks of life.

Then we understand why Jesus chose marriage as the sacrament to reflect his love for his Church. We realize that many marriages fail, that building a marriage and a family is difficult. But this underscores the greatness of good marriages, and if we appreciate this greatness, we will want to stand up and be counted with those who believe in marriage and work to build up the family.

### Marriage and the Bible (C 1609–17)

The greatness of marriage flows from the very nature of God. God is Father, Son, and Holy Spirit, a "family" of three Persons. Human beings are made in the image and likeness of God (Genesis 1:27), and because God is "family," men and women are called to create families. The three Persons of the Trinity love one another eternally, and people must love. God is creative, and people must share in God's creative action if human life is to continue.

Marriage, then, brings us close to the unity, love, and creativity of God. Old Testament writers expressed this fact in vivid imagery which married God to people: "For he who has become your husband is your Maker" (Isaiah 54:5). "On that day, says the LORD, she shall call me 'My husband'" (Hosea 2:18).

The New Testament portrays Christ as married to his Church. Paul writes, "I betrothed you to one husband to present you as a chaste virgin to Christ" (2 Corinthians 11:2). The union of Christ and his Church at the end of time is pictured as a wedding celebration: "For the wedding day of the Lamb has come, his bride has made herself ready" (Revelation 19:7). Marriage, of all human institutions, seems best suited to express the unity between God and us.

### Marriage as God's Design (C 1601–08)

Marriage is not merely a human institution; it comes from God: "God created man in his image; in the divine image he created him; male and female he created them. God blessed them, saying: 'Be fertile and multiply'" (Genesis 1:27-28).

Jesus clarified God's design for marriage in many ways. He was born into a human family, thereby showing the holiness of ordinary family life (Luke 2). He worked his first miracle at the wedding feast of Cana (John 2:1-11), putting the seal of God's approval on marriage: the love of husband and wife is worth celebrating! He taught that married love must be faithful: "You have heard that it was said, 'You shall not commit adultery.' But I say to you, everyone who looks at a woman with lust has already committed adultery with her in his heart" (Matthew 5:27-28). He proclaimed that married love should last forever: "From the beginning of creation, 'God made them male and female. For this reason a man shall leave his father and mother [and be joined to his wife], and the two shall become one flesh.' So they are no longer two but one flesh. Therefore what God has joined together, no human being must separate....Whoever divorces his wife and marries another commits adultery against her; and if she divorces her husband and marries another, she commits adultery" (Mark 10:6-12).

## Marriage in the Church (C 1621–54)

With such a background in Scripture, marriage should have been appreciated as a sacred and a sanctifying vocation by all followers of Christ. But some, influenced by philosophies regarding the soul as good and the body as bad, have taught that marriage is evil or, at best, only tolerable for the continuance of human life. Such attitudes had to be faced even in the New Testament era (1 Timothy 4:1-5), and they have resurfaced at various times through history. Vatican II stated the official position of the Church when it praised the goodness of family life and taught that married love is a sharing in God's love.

Marriage is a sacrament given to the Church by Christ. Christ did not create marriage after he became one of us, but he raised it to a new level. By participating in family life, by his presence at the wedding feast of Cana, and by his solemn declarations concerning the fidelity and permanence of marriage, Christ touched marriage with the grace of God in such a way that Paul could describe it as a great mystery "in reference to Christ and the church" (Ephesians 5:32).

So marriage is not just an arrangement between husband and wife. Every marriage affects others for good or ill. Each marriage is important to the children. A stable, loving marriage gives children an environment where they can mature into happy, loving adults; a marriage that is unhappy or shattered by divorce will be traumatic to them. Each marriage is important to the extended families of the couple. A happy marriage is a great blessing to parents and relatives. A marriage that fails, however, separates people from one another, creates pressures, sets up barriers between grandparents and grandchildren, and weakens the structures so necessary for happiness and peace.

Every marriage is important to God and the Church. "God is love" (1 John 4:16), but God depends on people to share love with others. Marriage and family life, as Ephesians 5:32 indicates, should show the world how Jesus loves his people. It is no exaggeration to say that Jesus depends largely on married couples for credibility in the world today. When a man and a woman stand before God on their wedding day and pledge their lives to each other, and then are faithful to their promises year after year, people take notice. They see Christ as the couple's source of strength and love. Christ's words at the Last Supper are verified: "This is how all will know that you are my disciples, if you have love for one another" (John 13:35). Christ's prayer at the Last Supper is answered: "I pray…that they may all be one, as you, Father, are in me and I in you, that they also may be in us, that the world may believe that you sent me" (John 17:20-21).

Because marriage has such important implications for the Church and for society as a whole, the Catholic Church has developed laws to safeguard the sacredness of marriage. Husband and wife must intend to be faithful, to make their marriage permanent, and to be open to the possibility of children. The "ministers" of the sacrament of matrimony are the bride and groom. A priest and two witnesses must be present, and it is through the vows and the presence of the community that Christ joins the husband and wife in love.

Interfaith marriages are common today, and engaged couples who are planning one should discuss areas such as worship, religious upbringing of children, and prayer. Catholics have a serious responsibility to share their faith with their children, and this may conflict with the partner's belief. Openness, prayer, and consultation are necessary in such cases. Interfaith marriages involving Catholics may be witnessed in a Catholic church. For a sufficient reason and with a dispensation from the bishop, they may be witnessed elsewhere.

Most dioceses have required programs designed to help couples prepare for marriage. Couples also meet with the parish priest to do necessary paperwork, plan the ceremony, and reflect upon the meaning of the sacrament. These preparations help couples make better decisions about marriage and can lead to stronger, healthier families.

After husband and wife make their vows, they continue to minister the grace of Christ to each other by every loving word and action. Their sacrament continues in all they do: work, play, communication, prayer, sexual intercourse, raising children, forgiveness, healing, social activities, all the ingredients of life. Married life, therefore, is a means by which Christ enters the home and fills it with his grace and love. Every Christian family should be a "little Church," a point of contact between God and people, so that family life can be the path of grace walked by most people to eternal life.

## Living the Ideal in the Real World (C 1646–66, 2204–33)

This is a very high ideal, and because we are human, we will not live it perfectly. But if couples appreciate the beauty and holiness of marriage, they are likely to do the practical things that make a marriage work. There are many fine books and resources available to help couples develop the skills necessary for marriage and family life. Couples must work at these skills, such as communication and child raising. A good marriage does not just "happen." It is built by love, prayer, attention, and constant effort.

Family counselors have observed that most marriages go through certain stages. First, there is the **honeymoon**, the rosy months when husband and wife see each other as perfect and are buoyed up by romantic feelings. Eventually, however, comes the second stage, **disillusionment**, as they begin to see the faults in each other, the same faults that exasperated their families before they married! This stage is followed by a third, **unhappiness**, as husband and wife wonder if it was a mistake to marry; they quarrel and try to change each other into the ideal they thought they had married in the first place. Many marriages break up at this point, often because unhappy couples do not realize that all people struggle with such problems. Couples who are realistic come to terms with the fact that no one is perfect, and each spouse learns to love the person he or she married, not the imaginary ideal of the romantic stage. This is the fourth stage of **acceptance**. Now husband and wife realize that their love is genuine, that they can depend on each other, that they are accepted and loved just as they are. This makes possible the fifth stage, the **happiness** each hoped for on their wedding day. Such stages may be repeated, as after the birth of a child or when the last child has left home. Couples who expect such patterns will not be surprised at disillusionment or pain and can work through these stages to real happiness.

Another fact basic to a successful marriage is that real love goes beyond emotions. Many people suppose that love is comprised of feelings of warmth and affection. Such emotions, often equated with "falling in love," make people feel good. However, these feelings inevitably pass, and when they do, many people quickly "fall out of love." Real love is a decision that endures even when romantic feelings are absent, the decision to put the good of the other on a par with one's own, to love the other as one's self. It includes many other decisions to be patient and kind, to put away selfishness, rudeness, and pride, to forgive and to endure (1 Corinthians 13).

For a successful marriage there must be good communication and mutual respect between husband and wife. The Bible says: "Be subordinate to one another out of reverence for Christ. Wives should be subordinate to their husbands as to the Lord. For the husband is head of his wife just as Christ is head of the church.... Husbands, love your wives, even as Christ loved the church and handed himself over for her" (Ephesians 5:21-25). This passage is sometimes construed to mean that the husband has the right of dominance over his wife. Not so. If wives are to be "subordinate to their husbands," then husbands are to love their wives "as Christ loved the church." Both wives and husbands are encouraged in Ephesians to give of themselves, generously and lovingly, in imitation of Christ.

When husband and wife are blessed with children, they have the first responsibility to teach them the gospel by word and example. Parents must spend time with their children, pray with them, talk to them about Jesus, instruct them about right and wrong, and live according to their beliefs. Parents must set priorities for important activities like family meals, working and playing together, and family discussions. In these and other ways, parents bring Christ into the home.

Some couples want children but cannot have them, and for this reason they bear the burden of disappointment and loss. Hopefully, such couples can find strength in the realization that their marital love is a great blessing to the whole Church. Their love can be fruitful, as they reach out and share that love with relatives, friends, and others.

### Resources for Growth in Married Love (C 1621, 1641–42)

Many professions and businesses offer programs to help people upgrade their skills. Marriage and family life require skills that are basic to happiness, and couples should put as much energy into upgrading family-life skills as they put into upgrading their abilities for work and business.

Every couple can benefit from the resources available through the Catholic Church and through other agencies. Marriage Encounter has been strengthening marriages all over the world. It teaches the beauty of sacramental marriage, as well as the communication skills that can make a good marriage better. Many dioceses and parishes offer marriage enrichment programs, counseling, and family-life seminars. Retreats for married couples and for families are available in most parts of the country. In recent years a new program has been developed to help save marriages of couples on the brink of separation or divorce. This program, *Retrouvaille* (the French word for rediscovery), has helped many couples find happiness and fulfillment in marriages once thought hopeless.

The most important resource for growth in married love is prayer. Research has shown that couples who worship together, read the Bible together, and pray together have an extremely high success rate in their marriages. There are many reasons for this. First, couples who seek from God the joy and peace that only God can give will not expect a spouse to be God! Human beings have longings in their hearts that can be filled by God alone. Those who expect them to be filled by a spouse will be disappointed. Second, marriage is built on love, and God is the source of all love. Married couples who fail to pray together on their pathway through life are like desert wanderers who die of thirst as they walk past springs of water. Third, couples who pray together express feelings that strengthen marriage and family life: gratitude, sorrow, forgiveness, praise, hope, and love. When a husband and wife, praying with each other, speak to God about such feelings, intimacy between the couple and God is strengthened.

## Marriage and Sexuality (C 1652–53, 2331–65)

The Book of Genesis teaches that God created man and woman, commanding them to "be fertile and multiply." The sexual nature of human beings, like all of God's creation, is "very good" (Genesis 1:28). The beauty of marital love is expressed in such books of the Bible as Ruth, Tobit, and the Song of Songs. As long as people have been on the earth, the sexual drive and the pleasure associated with it have brought men and women together to build homes and create families.

But if sexuality has great power for good when properly directed, it has the potential for creating tragedy and pain when misdirected. Sexuality then loses its connection with love and begets lust, which has wreaked havoc on human lives in every age. Lust can motivate the foulest treacheries, as when David murdered Uriah to steal his wife, Bathsheba (2 Samuel 11–12). Sexual activity, therefore, must be guided by God's laws, clearly expressed in the Bible.

"You shall not commit adultery." "You shall not covet your neighbor's wife." The sixth and ninth commandments (Exodus 20:14,17) forbid genital activity outside marriage. Jesus gave his followers even higher standards. He forbade divorce, teaching that husbands and wives must be faithful to each other forever (Mark 10:1-11). He said that "everyone who looks at a woman with lust has already committed adultery with her in his heart" (Matthew 5:28); he thus prohibited even lustful desires. Paul wrote: "Do not be deceived; neither fornicators nor idolaters nor boy prostitutes nor practicing homosexuals...will inherit the kingdom of God" (1 Corinthians 6:9-10). He further warned, "Be sure of this, that no immoral or impure or greedy person, that is, an idolater, has any inheritance in the kingdom of Christ and of God" (Ephesians 5:5; 1 Corinthians 6:15-20; Hebrews 13:4). These passages are very blunt in saying that genital sexual activity outside marriage excludes one from the kingdom of God.

The Bible forbids genital sexual activity outside marriage, not because sexuality is bad but because it is so good that it can have its fullest meaning only in marriage. Sexual intercourse is a means of communication, and God wants it to say: "I love you totally, faithfully, forever, and with openness to new life. You are the only person I love in this way." But intercourse can say many other things, like "I hate you" in rape, "Let's do business" in prostitution, "I like you but let's not get serious" in casual sex, or "I think I love you but let's try it for a while" in a living-together arrangement. Intercourse can communicate the very opposite of love, or less than it should, and so lose its power to express what God wants it to say. This perhaps explains why many married couples find sex boring or meaningless after a few years and why couples who live together before marriage have a higher divorce rate than those who do not. Genital sexual activity outside marriage is seriously sinful because it trivializes one of God's greatest gifts.

Many people of the twentieth century may think that such an approach to sexual *morality* is quaint and outmoded. On the contrary, sexual *immorality* is quaint and outmoded. The Greeks of Old Testament times and the pagans of New Testament times wallowed in immorality. Historians have observed that they, and all other societies that followed their example, were weakened and destroyed by the erosion of morality. Sexual immorality weakens individuals; many are the leaders who have fallen as a result of sexual indiscretions. Sexual immorality weakens families, and when the building blocks of society fail, society crumbles. Sexually transmitted diseases threaten civilization, today more than ever. History reveals that those who have been hurt by sexual immorality are countless. We will search in vain for any who have been helped by it. Countless are those who have benefited from following the standards of Christ. We will find no one hurt by them.

But tragically the modern media is largely controlled by individuals who deride the standards of Christ and promote sexual promiscuity. We who are Christian must have the courage to reject the "tired old sins" of the past and to walk in the light of the life-giving and love-giving principles of Jesus Christ.

## Catholic Family Planning (C 2366–79)

There are many movements today to avoid the artificial and seek out the natural. Many food additives are harmful. Many chemicals pollute the environment. Many artificial substances will be hazardous to living things long after they are disposed of. Aware of such problems, people are trying to live "in harmony with nature."

The official teaching of the Catholic Church on family planning would seem to fit very well with modern efforts to follow the patterns of nature. As presented by recent popes, Church teaching states that sexual intercourse has been given us by God to express love and to bring new human life into existence. To place an artificial barrier between the act and its natural result is to thwart God's purposes and is therefore wrong. The Church teaches that couples should plan their families, but they should use only natural means to do this.

In a world where "natural is beautiful," we might expect that the Church's teaching would find much support, but this has not been the case. After Vatican II many Catholics expected the Church to permit the use of artificial contraceptives. Pope Paul VI, however, in the encyclical letter *On Human Life* affirmed traditional Catholic teaching that has been strongly upheld by Pope John Paul II. The popular press has often presented papal teaching in negative fashion, influencing public opinion against an honest investigation into the values of natural family planning. Many Catholics, unaware of new natural methods and supposing the old "rhythm" approach to be the only one available, have not considered natural family planning as a viable option.

Yet Catholics who do follow the Church's teaching find that it has been a great blessing for marriage and family. The Couple to Couple League, a nonprofit organization founded in 1971, helps couples learn and practice the Sympto-Thermal Method of family planning. Couples using this method report that natural family planning benefits their marriages: It helps them become aware of their bodies and their natural fertility patterns, is very effective, keeps their sexual relationship alive, improves communication, and helps them understand the different needs of man and woman. Similar results are reported by couples using the Billings/Ovulation Method.

On the other hand, artificial methods of birth control have had some very negative results. There are serious health risks. IUDs (Intrauterine devices) have caused death and sterility. Medical reports show a higher incidence of cancer among women who use contraceptive pills, especially those who begin as teens or use the pill for a long time. If chemicals in vegetables, fruits, and animals can be dangerous to human beings, if people are concerned about side effects of medications, we may well wonder about the side effects of powerful drugs and chemicals whose whole purpose is to reverse the human reproductive process or render it ineffective. We may well wonder why more research has not been done to help couples determine when they are fertile, so that artificial means would be unnecessary.

Another negative effect of artificial methods of birth control is that they have placed emphasis more on the frequency of sexual acts than on their meaning. For many married couples sexual intercourse is not seen in its fullest meaning as an expression of love, and the emotional needs of spouses are neglected. A nationally syndicated columnist asked her women readers: "Would you be content to be held close and treated tenderly and forget about the act?" More than ninety thousand women responded; seventy-two percent said "yes." Obviously, for these women intercourse did not convey the love and affection they were looking for.

More sexual activity does not necessarily mean more happiness or better marriages. Since the advent of the pill, the divorce rate has increased, and there is evidence that infidelity among spouses is more common than it was fifty years ago. This does not mean that artificial birth control is the cause of divorce or infidelity, but it does indicate that couples who want successful marriages must look beyond mere sexual activity to other important issues.

Natural family planning includes discussion of such important issues. Couples who use natural family planning talk about the meaning of sexual intercourse. They weigh spiritual, emotional, and physical values. As a result, intercourse takes on new meaning, and their marriages are strengthened.

Catholic couples owe it to themselves to seriously examine the teaching of the Church on natural family planning and to study the natural methods available to them. Natural family planning is not always easy, but when people fit their lives into the patterns God has designed for life, they can expect God's blessings.

### Ceremony Without Marriage (C 1629)

Married life can bring happiness and meaning to life. Unfortunately, it can also end in betrayal, failure, broken homes, and broken hearts.

The Catholic Church believes that "what God has joined, no one may divide." But a man and woman can exchange vows and rings at a wedding without being joined by God. For a real marriage husband and wife must intend what God intends: that marriage be permanent, faithful, and open to children. They must be emotionally capable of such a marriage, and they must be free to marry.

Some people have intentions incompatible with Christian marriage. "I'll stay married if my spouse makes me happy; if not, we'll divorce." "No one person can keep another happy; therefore, we retain the right to have sex with other partners." "We will not have children because they interfere with the lifestyle we enjoy." The Catholic Church teaches that attitudes such as these "invalidate" a marriage, that is, they make a real marriage impossible.

A marriage ceremony is invalid if a spouse is incapable of entering into a loving union because of immaturity, psychological problems, or similar reasons, or if forced to marry. A ceremony is also invalid if one of the spouses is not free to marry because of a previous marriage or because marriage is forbidden by Church law or by a just civil law.

In these cases the wedding ceremony, even if Catholic, does not result in a valid marriage. Often such apparent marriages end in civil divorce, and one or both of the spouses may wish to marry in the Catholic Church. The official statement by the Church that no valid marriage existed between the two parties is called a declaration of nullity, or an annulment. An annulment is given by a diocesan tribunal, an office of the bishop, after a thorough investigation. It does not have civil effects and does not affect the legitimate status of children.

The Church may, on the authority of Paul (1 Corinthians 7:12-15), dissolve a marriage of unbaptized persons when one wishes to be baptized and the other refuses to live with the baptized person. This is called a "Pauline Privilege." The marriage of a baptized and an unbaptized person can also be dissolved under similar circumstances by the "Petrine Privilege," or "Privilege of the Faith."

The Catholic Church recognizes as valid the marriages of non-Catholics. In the eyes of the Church, civil divorce does not dissolve the marriages of Catholics or non-Catholics, although either may be declared invalid if the conditions for an annulment are present. Further, civil divorce does not exclude a Catholic from the practice of the faith. At times civil divorce may even be necessary to protect a spouse or children from abuse or mistreatment.

A person who wishes to inquire into the possibility of a declaration of nullity should contact a parish priest. Each diocese has its own procedures; the priest can explain these and help get the process started.

Many dioceses and parishes offer retreats and group experiences to help divorced individuals cope with their problems and live their faith. In these and in many other ways, the Catholic Church tries to show the compassion of Christ to those who have suffered from the trauma of divorce.

## Marriage and Eternal Life (C 1661)

The elderly gentleman who shared love and marriage with his wife for sixty years experienced the pain of parting as she died several years before he did. After her death he expressed confidence that he would join her again in heaven.

People often ask if husbands and wives will have a special relationship to each other after death. Some deny this, quoting Jesus' words: "When they rise from the dead, they neither marry nor are given in marriage, but they are like the angels in heaven" (Mark 12:25). But in this passage Jesus was simply meeting an objection to the resurrection placed by the Sadducees. His main point was that we do live after death. We will have spiritual bodies, "like the angels," and there will be no more death or birth. But the knowledge and love of this life will be intensified in the next, and surely God's love will keep us close to our loved ones.

Couples who walk down the aisle and through the pathways of this world together can look forward to walking hand in hand through the "new heaven and new earth," where God "will wipe every tear from their eyes, and there shall be no more death...or pain" (Revelation 21:1,4).

### Questions for Discussion or Reflection

Do you think that priests and religious should be "holier" than married people? Why or why not? Do you think that most married couples and families pray together often? What would be your reaction if you asked your priest when he prayed and his response was "Sundays and mealtimes?" What if you asked a married couple the same question and received the same answer? Is it possible to be a good priest or a good married couple without prayer?

### *Activities*

Couples should set aside time for prayer and should learn various ways of praying together. One fine method of praying is as follows:

1.  Let God speak to you. Read aloud a passage from the Bible. (One of the passages quoted above would be a good place to start.) Talk about it together and reflect on the passage until you come to a decision that makes a change for the better in your lives, like spending more time with each other.
2.  Pray out loud in your own words, talking to God about what is important to you and about anything suggested by the Scripture reading. This can include thanking and praising God, telling God of your love of God and each other, asking for help, asking pardon for failings. Focus on three areas of prayer: (a) yourselves, family and friends; (b) Church; and (c) world.
3.  Close with the prayer Jesus taught us, the Lord's Prayer. (Holding hands is a good way to express your unity in Christ.)

This prayer might take five minutes or an hour. There are many options for the second step, such as the "Lord, hear our prayer," a format used in the prayer of the faithful at Mass. And remember, God doesn't need elegant phrases, but just wants to talk with you as a couple!

# PART III
# CHRISTIAN LIFE

# CHAPTER FOURTEEN
## Morality—Jesus Guides Us Through Life

" **A** ctions speak louder than words." Study of our faith is meaningful only if it motivates us to act in a manner consistent with the teaching of Jesus. "What good is it, my brothers, if someone says he has faith but does not have works? Can that faith save him? If a brother or sister has nothing to wear and has no food for the day, and one of you says to them, 'Go in peace, keep warm, and eat well,' but you do not give them the necessities of the body, what good is it? So also faith of itself, if it does not have works, is dead" (James 2:14-17).

If we believe in Jesus Christ and accept the teaching of the Bible, we must translate our beliefs into action. In his Sermon on the Mount, Jesus said, "Not everyone who says to me, 'Lord, Lord,' will enter the kingdom of heaven, but only the one who does the will of my Father in heaven" (Matthew 7:21). We are brought to salvation by faith in Jesus Christ, but faith is more than an emotion or thought. Faith involves decisions and actions modeled on those of Jesus. Without faith in Christ we can do nothing good, but if we do nothing good, we cannot have faith in Christ! We will be judged according to our deeds (Revelation 20:12-13), and those in heaven are there because they have done good deeds in cooperation with God's grace (Revelation 19:8).

The teaching of Jesus demonstrates that we are free to make choices, that our choices should be in conformity with God's will, and that we are accountable for them. In making choices we are called to follow our conscience.

## Conscience (C 1776–1802, 1949–60)

Conscience is sometimes portrayed as a little angel hovering nearby, whispering what we should do and what we should avoid. But conscience is actually our sense of the moral goodness or evil of a thing. My conscience is myself, as I have the duty to listen to God, the ability to discern right or wrong, and the responsibility to choose what is right.

But how do we know what is right or wrong? Catholics believe that a true conscience must be in conformity with God's will. Something is right and moral if it is right in the eyes of God, wrong and immoral if it is wrong in the eyes of God. Some of the most basic notions of right and wrong are written by God in our hearts, as Paul says (Romans 2:15), but we must move beyond this "natural law" in our search to know God's will.

## Forming Our Conscience: The Bible (C 1783–85, 1961–64)

We begin by responding to the call of Jesus: "The kingdom of God is at hand. Repent, and believe in the gospel" (Mark 1:15). We consciously accept Jesus Christ as our guide, believing that his words and example teach us the best way to live. We study his teachings and apply them to the real decisions of daily life. In a practical way we look to Jesus for guidance in the choices we make in our personal lives, family, social circle, work, and civic duties.

Our source for the study of Christ's teachings is the Bible, and our starting point is the guideline that includes everything: love. "You shall love the Lord, your God, with all your heart, with all your soul, and with all your mind. This is the greatest and the first commandment. The second is like it: You shall love your neighbor as yourself. The whole law and the prophets depend on these two commandments" (Matthew 22:37-40; see Romans 13:8-10).

In making this statement, Jesus was echoing the Old Testament, for the "first commandment" is found in the Book of Deuteronomy (6:4-5) and the "second" in the Book of Leviticus (19:18). And when Jesus was asked by a young man, "What must I do to inherit eternal life?" he responded, "You know the commandments: 'You shall not kill; you shall not commit adultery; you shall not steal; you shall not bear false witness; you shall not defraud; honor your father and your mother' " (Mark 10:17-19). The moral teach-

ing of Jesus, then, includes an affirmation of these commandments of the Old Testament.

### The Ten Commandments (C 2052-57)

The Ten Commandments referred to by Jesus in the tenth chapter of Mark are the heart of Old Testament morality. The Jews
accepted them as God's will; they were expressed to Moses on
Mount Sinai (Exodus 20:1-20; Deuteronomy 5:1-21). They have
stood the test of time as standards of morality for countless generations.

Why are the commandments so significant? Because they can
make us truly free. The Israelites had been slaves in Egypt, and
once they had escaped from their bondage, God gave them the
commandments to safeguard them from falling into a worse slavery—that of sin. People who keep the commandments can enjoy
the full range of human freedom without being limited by the
restraints imposed by sin. Those who keep the first commandment will not be trapped by superstition. Those who keep the fourth
and sixth commandments will not through their own fault be en-
meshed in destructive family relationships.

If we are not truly free today, it is largely because the Ten Commandments are not obeyed. We must lock our possessions because
the seventh commandment is not kept. We fear to walk the streets
at night because the fifth commandment is not observed. The
worth of the commandments can be seen if we ask ourselves the
simple question, "What would the world be like tomorrow if everyone would do no more than keep the Ten Commandments?"

The commandments can also help us discern the true meaning
of love. *Love* is a word used in many ways, and we can deceive
ourselves into supposing that our choices arise from love when
they do not. The commandments make it clear that murder, adultery, theft, and the like are never the loving thing to do.

It is not possible in this chapter to discuss the full range of
meaning for each of the Ten Commandments. A listing of the commandments and some areas of morality they embrace may be found
in the examination of conscience in chapter ten. Reflection on
this examination can help us apply the commandments to our lives.
A detailed explanation of the commandments and of their application to modern life may be found in the *Catechism of the Catholic
Church*, 2052 to 2557.

## The Moral Teachings of Jesus (C 1965–86)

Jesus did more than affirm the Ten Commandments. He urged us to strive toward the higher standard: "You have heard that it was said to your ancestors, 'You shall not kill; and whoever kills will be liable to judgment.' But I say to you, whoever is angry with his brother will be liable to judgment" (Matthew 5:21-22). He said that we must avoid lustful thoughts, not just adultery. Old patterns allowing divorce, revenge, and hatred must be abandoned. What was the higher standard given by Jesus? "Be perfect, just as your heavenly Father is perfect" (Matthew 5:48).

Jesus revised the way people were to look at contemporary moral guidelines. The Pharisees of Jesus' time imposed stringent requirements on people with their legal interpretations. When Jesus' disciples were hungry and began to pick heads of grain and eat them, the Pharisees accused them of harvesting, forbidden on the Sabbath (Exodus 34:21). Jesus defended his followers on the principle that the Sabbath was made for people and not people for the Sabbath (Mark 2:23-28). Jesus repudiated the narrowness of the Pharisees and taught that the good of humans must come before mere legalism.

Jesus condemned some legal interpretations then in vogue. He attacked the Pharisees because they allowed people to "dedicate" funds to the Temple, meaning that they could use the funds for themselves but not for others, even needy parents! Jesus made it clear that we must always interpret the commandments according to a genuine spirit of love for God and others (Mark 7:8-13).

Jesus nullified portions of the old law. The Old Testament designated some foods as clean and others as unclean—not to be eaten. Jesus explained that what we eat cannot make us unclean, but that the thoughts, words, and deeds which come from our hearts can. "Thus he declared all foods clean" (Mark 7:19). It took the followers of Jesus a long time to understand what this meant, but eventually the early Church felt free to withdraw from Jewish dietary bans and from such important Jewish practices as circumcision (Acts 15). This had profound implications upon moral judgments made by Christians from that time on.

Whether Jesus was teaching that true justice went beyond Old Testament standards in matters like divorce or that dietary regulations no longer applied, he was urging us to move beyond legalism to what truly fosters love. He said, "Do not think that I have come to abolish the law or the prophets. I have come not to abolish but to fulfill" (Matthew 5:17). Laws are necessary and good, but Christ's followers must constantly strive to view them according to their mind and heart.

### The Church (C 2030–51)

Catholics believe that we have another resource available to us as we form our consciences: the teachings of the Church. Jesus is present in his Church and has given its leaders the authority to speak and act in his name. "Whatever you bind on earth," he said to Peter, "shall be bound in heaven; and whatever you loose on earth shall be loosed in heaven" (Matthew 16:19).

Jesus told his disciples to go to all nations, "teaching them to observe all that I have commanded" (Matthew 28:20). After his Ascension the apostles applied the commands of Jesus to the situations they encountered. Thus, guided by the Holy Spirit, they decreed that Christians in Antioch were not bound by Jewish law but did impose a few limitations for the sake of good order (Acts 15). As circumstances changed, even those limitations were dropped.

New Testament Christians looked to their leaders for guidance in moral questions, as when the Corinthians wrote to Paul for advice (1 Corinthians 7:1). Paul issued directives for them concerning such issues as marriage, foods sacrificed to idols, and behavior in liturgical assemblies. All New Testament letters offered moral guidance, and some, notably the pastoral letters, gave rules of conduct in matters of church organization, relationships, and daily life.

Since then the Catholic Church has provided moral leadership for its members through laws and instruction from pastors, bishops, and popes. Circumstances change with time, and people today face moral problems undreamed of by first-century Christians. Church leaders are responsible for teaching how the gospel applies to modern life and for giving us laws to guide us. The most significant of these are found in *The Code of Canon Law* (a collection of laws for the Church). Important also are the "Precepts of the Church," which oblige Catholics to attend Mass on Sundays and holy days, confess sins at least once a year, receive Communion during the Easter season, observe the prescribed days of fasting and abstinence, and support the Church according to our abilities.

Catholics should give serious consideration to Church laws and to its teaching. Leaders today can make mistakes, just as the apostles could (Galatians 2:11-14), but the pope and the bishops possess a special authority from Christ that should not be taken lightly.

## The Teaching of Theologians
## and Common Practice of Good Catholics (C 2033-40)

Throughout Church history there have been great teachers of moral theology (the study of morality) like Saint Thomas Aquinas and Saint Alphonsus Liguori and great masters of the spiritual life like Saint Teresa and Saint John of the Cross. Their writings have helped form the consciences of generations of Catholics, and they have established moral principles that have been useful for centuries. Today there are theologians and spiritual writers who are especially qualified to offer moral guidance by reason of their education and experience. When we are faced with difficult moral decisions, moral theologians and spiritual advisers, past and present, can render valuable assistance and guidance. The common practice of good Catholics who are led by the Holy Spirit can also guide us. Much of our appreciation of the goodness of marital sexual relationships, for example, comes from the experience of good Catholics.

## A Good Conscience (C 1730–75)

The teachings of Jesus Christ and of the Bible, the guidance of the Church, the instructions of moral theologians, and experience are the sources available to us as we strive to form a good conscience. They provide us with objective guidelines so that our decisions are not merely subjective and emotional. In some cases we may find the right course of action quickly and easily. For instance, the teaching of Jesus and the Bible, the moral directives of the Church, the teachings of good theologians, and experience are one in telling us that it is evil to murder an innocent person. In other cases the answers are not so clear. Is it permissible to kill someone who is attacking an innocent person? If so, under what circumstances? Here a great deal of study may be required.

Catholics should be aware of proper moral guidelines. They should know which areas of morality allow for flexibility and which areas demand a specific response. In some cases Catholics may freely choose between several alternatives without sin because the issue has not been clearly resolved. Thus one Catholic might choose to serve as a soldier, while another might feel obliged to serve only in a nonaggressive capacity. In other cases Catholics may not licitly make some choices because these violate the clear teaching of the Bible and of the Church. Abortion is such a case, and Catholics who take part in an abortion or promote abortions are transgressing the law of God in a serious matter.

### Becoming More Christlike in Our Moral Choices (C 1877–1948)

It is possible in the study of moral theology to make the mistake of assuming that our main goal in life is the avoidance of sin. Our real goal, however, is to become more like Jesus Christ, to act out of love rather than out of a sense of obligation. A mother will make great sacrifices for her infant, lavishing care both day and night. She does so gladly out of love and goes to extremes of service she might never approach if she were working for pay. So, too, love is a "law without limits," and if we strive to love as Christ loves, we are likely not only to keep the commandments but to go far beyond them in our service of God and neighbor.

The love of Christ will always challenge us to work for peace and social justice and to have a special concern for the poor. Christ cautioned us that our eternal destiny will be determined by our readiness to help others and reminded us that whatever we do for others is done for him (Matthew 25:31-46).

Christ's love will also challenge us to be consistent in our moral choices. Some people are generous and loving to people they visit at a nursing home, but thoughtless and unkind toward members of their own families. Some use their tongue to praise God in church, then fall into habits of cursing and gossiping in the workplace (James 3:1-12). "Love never fails" (1 Corinthians 13:8).

### Sin and Grace (C 1846–76, 1987–2011)

The Bible teaches that sin goes back to the first human beings on earth. The story of Adam and Eve shows how people rejected God, choosing their own definitions of right and wrong. Through Adam and Eve, sin entered the world, separating us from the fullness of God's grace, weakening our ability to overcome sin, and subjecting us to the dominion of death. This "fallen state" is called *original sin*. It does not make human nature evil, but damages it. Original sin has affected all human beings, with the exception of Jesus and Mary.

The Church teaches that the effects of original sin are countered by baptism. This sacrament rejoins us to God, who then dwells within us as a Friend. Baptism bestows *sanctifying grace*, God's life and love making us sons and daughters in the Trinitarian family. Baptism does not remove our tendencies to sin, but gives us access to the helping grace of God called *actual grace*. Sanctifying grace may be compared to the love parents have for their children. Actual grace may be compared to the many acts of love parents perform for their children like feeding, clothing, and teaching them. Baptized, we have sanctifying and actual grace to help us live a morally good life. But we must also struggle against the weaknesses of human nature and against the temptations that attract us to evil.

When we choose evil, acting against our consciences, we commit what is called *actual* or *personal sin*. Sin begins in our free will, as we choose to act in a way contrary to God's will. Sin may find expression in actions whether external, such as murder or theft, or internal, such as lustful thoughts, envy, or hatred. Sin may find expression also in omissions when we fail to do what we ought, as when we neglect the poor or fail to worship God.

Sin can exist in different degrees. We may be trying to follow Christ and direct our lives in accord with God's commandments so that our fundamental direction is toward God. But we can do something wrong or fail to do what is right because we are weak or selfish. If our failing is of such a nature that it does not sever our bond of love with God, it is known as *venial sin*. Examples of such sins might be carelessness in prayer, unkind words, and bouts of temper. These sins may be venial, but we should try to overcome them, for just as minor failings can damage our relationship with others, so venial sins can weaken our friendship with God and lead to more serious failings.

There are sins which are so serious that they reverse the course of our lives, turning us away from God, changing our fundamental direction toward sin and death. These are called *mortal sins*, sins that are deadly because they cut us off from God's love. (Mortal sins are often referred to as *serious sins*). Paul gives examples of such sins: "Now the works of the flesh are obvious: immorality, impurity, licentiousness, idolatry, sorcery, hatreds, rivalry, jealousy, outbursts of fury, acts of selfishness, dissensions, factions, occasions of envy, drinking bouts, orgies, and the like. I warn you, as I warned you before, that those who do such things will not inherit the kingdom of God" (Galatians 5:19-21). This is not a complete list, and some of these sins can be less serious at times, as when we are selfish in a light matter. But Paul clearly indicates the existence of sins so serious that they exclude us from the kingdom of God.

It is not possible to establish precise guidelines that would determine in every case whether a given sin is mortal or venial. Some sins are obviously mortal, such as murder and adultery, while others are obviously venial, such as little acts of disobedience by a small child. Others can leave doubt. It would be a venial sin for a child to steal a piece of candy from a store and (objectively, at least) a mortal sin for a thief to steal a poor widow's life savings. But we cannot so easily determine degrees of guilt between these two extremes.

Theologians explain that three conditions must be present for a mortal sin. First, there must be *serious matter*, something that causes serious harm to others or ourselves or is a serious affront to God. Second, there must be *sufficient reflection*: the sinner must be fully aware of the wickedness of the action. Most small children do not have the mental capacity to comprehend the evil of sin and so could not commit a mortal sin. Adults who are mentally deficient or who have had no opportunity to learn about right and wrong might also be incapable of mortal sin. Third, there must be *full consent of the will*: the sinner must freely choose to do what is evil. A man forced to steal money because his child is being held hostage would not have true freedom. Some people can be so damaged emotionally by background or illness that they do not have the freedom or moral maturity necessary to commit mortal sin. But when all three conditions—serious matter, sufficient reflection, and full consent of the will—are present, mortal sin exists.

## God's Gift to Us and Our Gift to God (C 1803–45)

Life and freedom are God's gifts to us; what we become through our use of freedom is our gift to God. God places us on this earth and invites us to love and serve our Creator, opening ourselves to God's love for all eternity. Each day we are given life and freedom. Each day we determine the kind of person we will become. On the one hand we have the grace of God assisting us to make the right decisions. On the other hand we are tempted by the devil, by people who sin, and by our own inborn weaknesses. When we make our choices in accord with the dictates of a properly formed conscience, we lead a morally good life. When we go against the moral guidelines given by God, we sin.

The more we choose a certain course or way of acting, whether good or bad, the easier it becomes to perform that action. Thus we form either good habits, called *virtues*, or bad habits, called *vices*. The more we speak with kindness and gentleness, the more readily kind words come to our lips. The more we curse or gossip, the more these vices become ingrained in us.

Catholic tradition has assigned special importance to certain virtues. Foremost are faith, hope, and love, called the "theological virtues" because they are gifts of God and direct our relationship to God. By *faith* we acknowledge the reality of God in our lives and are able to believe in the truths that God reveals to us. By *hope* we have confident assurance of achieving our eternal goal with the help of God's grace. By *love* we make the decision to put God first with all our heart, soul, mind, and strength, and to love our neighbor as ourselves. While these virtues are gifts of God, we must be willing to accept them from God and to live in such a way that they can grow stronger in us.

There are vices that oppose the theological virtues. We sin against faith by choosing such false gods as materialism, astrology, or superstition, or by failing to pray, or study our religion. (Doubts against faith do not necessarily mean the loss of faith, for we will experience temptations against faith just as we do against other virtues.) Sins against hope are presumption, by which we attempt to live without reference to God, and despair, by which we renounce trust in God. (Sometimes despair can originate in depression or emotional illness rather than in a deliberate sinful choice.) Sins against love include hatred of God (as in Satanism), sloth (the neglect of God and of spiritual things), and failure to love our neighbor (1 John 4:20-21).

We grow in the theological virtues by turning to God often in prayer, participating in the Mass and sacraments, making acts of faith, hope, and love (see Activities section), and asking God to strengthen us in these virtues. Study of the Bible and Catholic teaching will fortify faith, hope, and love, as will exercise of these virtues. When we struggle against doubt, despair, or spiritual dryness, and act in faithful, hopeful, loving ways, we allow God to strengthen us in the theological virtues.

Other virtues which have a special place in Catholic tradition are the four *moral* virtues, also called the *cardinal* virtues (from the Latin word for "hinge") because so many other virtues "hinge" on them. *Prudence* helps us to do the right thing in any circumstance. *Justice* enables us to give others their due. *Fortitude* strengthens us to weather the difficulties and temptations of life. *Temperance* helps us to control our desires and to use the good things of life in a Christlike way. The gifts and fruits of the Holy Spirit (see page 97) are prominent in Christian spirituality. Many other virtues like humility are taught in the Bible; attentiveness to God's Word will help us become familiar with them.

Catholic tradition recognizes certain vices as especially significant because they are at the heart of most sinful decisions. These are the *seven deadly sins*: pride, greed, lust, anger, gluttony, envy, and sloth. When we find evidence of such sins in our lives, we can uproot them by sincere repentance, by turning to Christ in the sacrament of penance, and by practicing the virtues contrary to them.

Saint Paul describes Christian life as a process by which we turn away from sin and put on the virtues of Christ. "Put to death, then, the parts of you that are earthly: immorality, impurity, passion, evil desire, and the greed that is idolatry....You must put them all away: anger, fury, malice, slander, and obscene language out of your mouths. Stop lying to one another, since you have taken off the old self with its practices and have put on the new self, which is being renewed, for knowledge, in the image of its creator....Put on then, as God's chosen ones, holy and beloved, heartfelt compassion, kindness, humility, gentleness, and patience, bearing with one another and forgiving one another, if one has a grievance against another; as the Lord has forgiven you, so must you also do. And over all these put on love, that is, the bond of perfection. And let the peace of Christ control your hearts....And whatever you do, in word or in deed, do everything in the name of the Lord Jesus, giving thanks to God the Father through him" (Colossians 3:5,8-10,12-15,17).

## The Imitation of Christ (C 1691-98, 2012-29)

When we speak of morality, of moral theology, of freedom and conscience, of observing the commandments, of living in grace instead of in sin, of choosing virtue over vice, we can sum it all up in Paul's phrase, "Life is Christ" (Philippians 1:21). Life for us should be a constant effort to be one with Jesus, making our everyday decisions according to his mind and heart. We should treat the members of our family with kindness because we believe in Jesus. The way we relate to our friends, coworkers, and people on the street should be a result of our relationship with Christ. The books we read, the television shows and movies we watch, the language we use, the clothes we wear, should be in accord with our life in Christ. Our business decisions, political choices, and social relationships should be, insofar as possible, in harmony with what Christ would do if he were in our place.

Living our life in harmony with the love of Christ may put us at odds with secular society. At times we may make choices that will cause others to ask, "Why are they acting in that way?" with the only satisfactory answer being, "Because they believe in Jesus Christ." Actions do speak louder than words, and we should reflect often on a brief and humorous "examination of conscience" expressed in the question, "If you were arrested for being a Christian, would there be enough evidence to convict you?"

### *Questions for Discussion or Reflection*

Can you name the Ten Commandments? Using the examination of conscience based on the Ten Commandments (chapter ten) as a guide, how many sins can you name that are forbidden by each commandment? How many virtues can you name that are counseled by each commandment? What would the world be like if everyone would keep the Ten Commandments?

### *Activities*

Sincere individuals sometimes **want** to believe in God, but seem to be shackled by doubts and fears. Faith is a gift from God, and so we should ask for it. Faith is also a human act, which means that we should do our part: study the truths of Catholicism, read the Scriptures, and try to imitate Jesus in our actions. Each time we pray the Creed or make an Act of Faith (see below) we not only profess our faith; we also seek the grace of a stronger faith. "Lord, I believe. Help my unbelief!"

Meditate on the following New Testament passage: "Examine yourselves to see whether you are living in faith. Test yourselves. Do you not realize that Jesus Christ is in you?" (2 Corinthians 13:5).

*You may wish to memorize the following prayers:*

### *Act of Faith*

O my God, I firmly believe that you are one God in three divine Persons, Father, Son, and Holy Spirit; I believe that your divine Son became man and died for our sins, and that he will come to judge the living and the dead. I believe these and all the truths which the holy Catholic Church teaches, because you revealed them, who can neither deceive nor be deceived. Amen.

### *Act of Hope*

O my God, relying on your infinite goodness and promises, I hope to obtain pardon of my sins, the help of your grace, and life everlasting, through the merits of Jesus Christ, my Lord and Redeemer. Amen.

### *Act of Love*

O my God, I love you above all things, with my whole heart and soul, because you are all good and worthy of all my love. I love my neighbor as myself for the love of you. I forgive all who have injured me and I ask pardon of all whom I have injured. Amen.

# PART IV
# PRAYER

# CHAPTER FIFTEEN
## Communicating With God—Prayer

O n August 20, 1977, the spacecraft *Voyager 2* was launched from Earth to explore our solar system and send back information about some of its planets and moons. After visiting Neptune in 1989, *Voyager* flew at thirty-seven thousand miles an hour into the vast reaches of the universe, carrying a message, a twelve-inch gold-plated disk with sounds and images from Earth. It is exciting to think that someday other intelligent beings might "get the message" and send a response to us.

It is far more exciting to realize that we human beings can exchange messages, not just with other creatures but with the Creator of the universe! Communication with God—prayer—can be one of the most interesting and fulfilling experiences of human existence. But we do not first send a message and wait for a reply, as we have done with *Voyager 2*. Prayer begins with God.

### Close Encounters (C 2558–67)

In the science fiction movie *Close Encounters of the Third Kind* people from many places and walks of life suddenly received a mental image of a certain mountain in the western United States. Without knowing why, they painted pictures and produced clay moldings of the mountain and felt a need to find this place they had never seen. Gradually, some of them began to meet one another and share experiences. They came to the realization that intelligent beings from outer space had communicated with them. They learned to exchange information with those beings through light and music and eventually achieved a "close encounter of the third kind," a face-to-face meeting, and received an invitation to visit their world.

This science fiction story may be seen as a pattern for prayer. God has spoken in various ways to all human beings, imprinting messages in our minds and hearts. When we share our experiences with one another, we come to realize that our Creator is calling us. We learn to listen and to speak to God in many ways (including light and music!). We achieve the "close encounter" of prayer and receive an invitation from God to enter "new heavens and a new earth."

Prayer "happens" when we open our senses, minds, wills, and hearts to the many ways God speaks to us. We reflect on God's Word, letting it touch our hearts. We then respond to God. As we do, we look to the Bible for guidance.

### Prayer in the Old Testament (C 2568–97)

God placed human beings on this earth and invited them to respond. God is not a distant Power but a loving Creator who speaks to those made "in his image" (Genesis 1:27). Unfortunately, sin causes people to distance themselves from God; Adam and Eve "hid themselves from the LORD God" (Genesis 3:8). God never stopped reaching out to people, however, and when anyone listened, communication with God resumed. Abraham began the Jewish tradition of prayer (Genesis 12–25). Moses encountered God in a burning bush (Exodus 3), in the crossing of the Red Sea (Exodus 14), in the thunder of Mount Sinai (Exodus 20), and in the intimacy of the meeting tent (Exodus 33). David heard God calling him to repentance and responded with prayer, fasting, and penance (2 Samuel 12). Solomon built a Temple to the Lord and led his people in a public prayer of praise and petition (1 Kings 8). The prophets, who spoke for God, also spoke with God. Elijah found God in a "tiny whispering sound" (1 Kings 19:12). Isaiah showed that holiness is required for real prayer (Isaiah 1). Jeremiah expressed his deepest feelings to God in prayer (Jeremiah 20:7-18). The Wisdom Books recommend prayer and give beautiful patterns of prayer (Sirach 17:19-27; 36). The Book of Psalms is a collection of prayers for all occasions.

We can learn much about prayer from the Old Testament and find prayers to suit every situation. For thousands of years, people have found comfort in prayers like Psalm 23:1: "The LORD is my shepherd." But Old Testament prayer has limitations. It sometimes reflects a spirit of vengeance: "O God, smash their teeth in their mouths" (Psalm 58:7); and a spirit of ruthlessness and cruelty: "Fair Babylon, you destroyer, happy those…who seize your children and smash them against a rock" (Psalm 137:8-9). We may "skip over" such prayers, seeing them as expressions of a limited theology. For the perfection of prayer, we move to the New Testament and the prayer of Jesus.

## The Prayer of Jesus (C 2598–2616, 2759–2865)

Jesus was both God and human, and it may not be easy for us to understand how he could pray. Did he pray as a human being and answer his own prayer as God? We can never fully grasp the mystery of Jesus' prayer any more than we can fully understand the mystery of the Incarnation, but we can be sure that the divine consciousness did not negate the human consciousness of Jesus. Jesus "advanced in wisdom and age and favor before God and man" (Luke 2:52), and prayer must have been a part of the process by which he knew God as his Father (Luke 2:49) and himself as the "beloved Son" (Luke 3:22). Jesus prayed for the same reason we do, to communicate with God. But his prayer was perfect, and so, like the apostles, we turn to him and ask, "Lord, teach us to pray" (Luke 11:1).

When we look at the prayer of Jesus, we discover that it was as natural to him as breathing. He began his public life with prayer (Luke 3:22), then went into the desert to spend forty days in communion with God (Matthew 4:1-11). He prayed often and long during his ministry, even at the busiest times (Mark 1:35; 6:45-56). He sought guidance from God before making important decisions, like choosing the Twelve Apostles (Luke 6:12-16). His union with his Father could be so intense that it left his disciples awestruck (Luke 9:28-36). He prayed for himself in time of distress (Hebrews 5:7-8), and he prayed for his apostles (Luke 22:31-34). He participated in official Jewish worship (Luke 22:7-9). He prayed in synagogues (Mark 1:21-22) and in the Jerusalem Temple (Luke 2:41-52).

We can pray the words of Jesus as recorded in the New Testament. In the Lord's Prayer, Jesus taught us to call God "our Father" (Matthew 6:9). In other prayers, Jesus praised God for having revealed his mysteries to the childlike (Matthew 11:25-26), thanked God just before he raised Lazarus from the dead (John 11:41-42), and interceded for the disciples and for us (John 17).

When troubled Jesus prayed to his Father (John 12: 27-28), and in his agony he prayed at Gethsemane (Matthew 26:36-44). In prayers said from the cross, Jesus expressed his feelings of desolation (Matthew 27:46), forgave those who persecuted him (Luke 23:34), and commended his spirit into the hands of his Father (Luke 23:46). We can praise and thank God, ask forgiveness, and make requests in prayers said by Christ. It is comforting to know that even when we find it hardest to pray, when we feel abandoned or overwhelmed or at the very threshold of death, Jesus gives us words to speak to our heavenly Father.

Looking beyond the actual prayers said by Jesus, we find that he taught a great deal about prayer. In the Sermon on the Mount, Jesus tells us that we must pray with sincerity, not to impress others; we must avoid the pagan attitude that God owes us a response in proportion to the length of our prayers. Our Father knows what we need before we ask; therefore, the purpose of prayer is to express our dependence upon God, as in the Lord's Prayer, where we put present ("Give us this day our daily bread"), past ("forgive us our trespasses"), and future ("deliver us from evil") in God's hands (Matthew 6:5-15). Prerequisites for prayer are humility (Luke 18:9-14) and forgiveness of others (Mark 11: 25-26).

We should pray with faith and confidence, for prayer is always answered: "Therefore, I tell you, all that you ask for in prayer, believe that you will receive it and it shall be yours" (Mark 11:24); "Ask and it will be given to you; seek and you will find; knock and the door will be opened to you" (Matthew 7:7). There is a special power in common prayer: "Amen, [amen,] I say to you, if two of you agree on earth about anything for which they are to pray, it shall be granted to them by my heavenly Father" (Matthew 18:19).

If we read only the passages in the previous paragraph, however, we can get a one-sided view of Jesus' teaching on prayer. We have all had the experience of asking and *not* receiving. Because of this we can get discouraged and give up on prayer, or feel guilty, thinking we lack faith. But these passages must be interpreted in the light of Jesus' other teachings about prayer.

To begin with, Jesus implies that God's answer to prayer may take time, for perseverance in prayer is necessary (Luke 11:5-13; 18:1-8). Jesus also shows us that our prayer must always be made in accordance with God's will. In the Garden of Gethsemane, Jesus prayed, "My Father, if it is possible, let this cup pass from me; yet, not as I will, but as you will" (Matthew 26:39). "Thy will be done" must be the foundation of every prayer we say.

The perfect submission of Jesus to God's will was part of his every prayer. When Jesus tells us, "Whatever you ask in my name, I will do" (John 14:13), we can be sure that praying in his name includes the condition, "If this is God's will." When Jesus says, "If you remain in me and my words remain in you, ask for whatever you want and it will be done for you" (John 15:7), we must remember that Jesus, in whom we "remain," endured the agony of Gethsemane, and his words which "remain" in us include "not as I will, but as you will."

## Other New Testament Teachings About Prayer (C 2617–49)

We learn from the New Testament how to pray in the spirit of the first Christians. Prayer is, above all, Trinitarian. God is to be addressed personally as our dear Father (Romans 8:15). We pray to the Father "through Jesus Christ" (Romans 1:8), who always intercedes for us (Hebrews 7:25). The Holy Spirit lives in us and helps us pray, for "we do not know how to pray as we ought, but the Spirit himself intercedes with inexpressible groanings" (Romans 8:26).

The New Testament encourages us to pray constantly (Ephesians 6:18), in common with others (Acts 2:42), and in song (Colossians 3:16). Prayer may be praise (Romans 14:11), thanks (Colossians 3:17), sorrow for sin (James 5:16), and petition (Philippians 4:6). Prayer intentions include a safe journey (Romans 1:10), salvation of others (Romans 10:1), deliverance from enemies (Romans 15:31), spiritual needs (Ephesians 3:14-21), and peace (1 Timothy 2:1-4). In time of special need, fasting may accompany prayer (Luke 2:37; Acts 13:2-3; 14:23).

We can pray in the very words placed on the lips of Mary (Luke 1:46-55), Zachary (Luke 1:68-79), and Simeon (Luke 2:29-32). We can make our own the brief prayers found throughout the gospels, like that of the distraught father, "I do believe, help my unbelief" (Mark 9:24), and of Bartimeus, "Jesus, son of David, have pity on me" (Mark 10:48). Paul gives us many beautiful prayers (Romans 11:33-36; 2 Corinthians 1:3-4) and magnificent hymns of praise (Ephesians 1:3-10; Philippians 2:5-11; Colossians 1:15-20). Many other examples of New Testament prayers may be found (for example, 1 Peter 1:3-5; Revelation 4:11).

## Catholic Prayer (C 2650–62)

The Scriptures open up many pathways to prayer. Instructed by the Old and New Testaments, and guided by the Holy Spirit, Catholics have listened to the voice of God and responded in many ways. Catholics have encountered God in thunder and storm as did Moses and in the gentle breeze like Elijah. They have gone into the desert like Jesus to find God in solitude and silence, and they have prayed together as did the early Christians.

Catholics have meditated upon God's actions in their lives like Mary (Luke 2:52), and they have voiced the psalms and the Lord's Prayer. They have offered up their work in the morning and asked forgiveness at night. They have looked at the crucifix and joined their sufferings to those of Christ. They have fasted and made pilgrimages, breathed the name of Jesus and recited long litanies, fingered rosary beads and savored the fragrance of incense, walked the Stations of the Cross and knelt in silence. They have prayed in joy at the birth of a child and in tears at the death of a friend. In restaurants and at picnics, Catholics have said grace before meals. They have made the Sign of the Cross in churches and on baseball diamonds. In great cathedrals glittering with stained glass and in tiny roadside chapels, they have "raised their minds and hearts to God."

Our Catholic tradition is rich and varied. It offers us limitless possibilities for prayer and encourages us to make prayer a part of life. As an aid to this, we offer some "pathways to prayer" and some attitudes toward prayer.

## Pathways to Prayer: God Speaks to Us (C 2663–82)

Prayer is not something we initiate. God has already started the conversation. But how does God "speak" to us? Perhaps some comparisons with human communication will be helpful.

We use words to communicate, but we convey thoughts and feelings in many other ways. Parents often say their first "words" of love to newborn children with a hug and a kiss. Parents "speak of" care and security to their children by clothing and feeding them. All of us speak with "body language," with facial expressions, with gifts and acts of love, even with silence. We learn to communicate also by evoking the memory of others, by stirring up their emotions, by stimulating their intellect, by touching their imagination, and by encouraging them to act. God communicates with us in all these ways, and more.

- God addressed us at the moment of our conception. What God spoke to Jeremiah he could say to every human being, "Before I formed you in the womb I knew you" (Jeremiah 1:5). God gives life to each of us and so invites us to respond to divine creative love.
- God speaks to us through the universe. Every good and beautiful thing is a word spoken to us by the Creator. "The heavens declare the glory of God" (Psalm 19:2). "For from the greatness and beauty of created things their original author, by analogy, is seen" (Wisdom 13:5; see Romans 1:20).
- God speaks to us through the events in our lives, by providential care. "The LORD is my shepherd....He guides me in right paths" (Psalm 23:1,3).
- God speaks to us through the Bible, which is always "living and effective, sharper than any two-edged sword, penetrating even between soul and spirit, joints and marrow, and able to discern reflections and thoughts of the heart" (Hebrews 4:12).
- God speaks to us through people like the prophets (Matthew 1:22; Acts 3:18). Above all, God speaks to us through Jesus Christ (Hebrews 1:1-2). Jesus is "the Word" of God: "In the beginning was the Word, and the Word was with God, and the Word was God....And the Word became flesh" (John 1:1,14).
- God also can address us by evoking memories, by stirring up emotions, by stimulating thoughts and images, and by encouraging us to act. God can use these doorways to our consciousness, memory, emotions, intellect, imagination, and will, for God created them! When we are quiet, we can learn to hear God's voice in the memories, feelings, thoughts, images, and decisions that arise in us. How do we know that they are of God and not just products of our imaginations? When they are of God, they will be in accord with the teachings of Scripture and the Church, and will produce the good fruits of love,

service, generosity, and peace. In difficult matters, we may consult with a spiritual adviser.

Beyond the ordinary experiences of prayer, many people have reported visions of Christ, Mary, angels, or saints. The Catholic Church is very cautious about verifying such visions, but in some cases has declared some—like those at Fatima and Lourdes—as worthy of belief. Visions and voices are not essential for prayer, and many of the greatest saints never had such experiences.

## Pathways to Prayer: Attentiveness to God (C 2683–96)

We have said that God speaks with us through the words of the Bible. Are we attentive to God's voice when the Bible is proclaimed at Mass? Do we often read the Bible with eagerness to hear what God says to us, especially through Jesus?

We must become attentive to God's many other "words" of love. What does God say to us at every moment by the very fact that God has created us and holds us in being? What do God's gifts of sunshine and air, sound and color, scent and taste, warmth and cold, light and darkness, say to us? What does God say by giving us family and friends, food and shelter, mountains and seas, forests and plains? Have we learned to feel the gentle caress of God in a warm breeze? Do we experience God's power in the storm, God's magnificence in the starry night? Do we sense the presence of God in the goodness of human beings, especially in the kindnesses they show us? Are we aware of this "body language" of God?

Do we allow God to speak to our mind, emotions, imagination, memory, and will? Do we give God our full attention so that God can call forth ideas into our intellect, fill our heart with love, touch us with images that console and encourage, help us to remember the great things God has done for us, and challenge us to make decisions?

We will hear God speaking only if we become attentive. Scientists have set up huge radio antennas that are constantly "listening" for any signal from outer space. We need to tune the "antennas" of our minds and hearts to God. This is not easy. Our lives are always busy and often hectic.

First, we must find time. Some people rise early to pray for an hour, half-hour, or fifteen minutes. Others pray during lunch hour or just before retiring. The important thing is to schedule time for prayer and be faithful to it. If we can't find fifteen minutes, then we should set aside five, or even one. Better to pray one minute a day than to pray not at all because we "can't find the time."

After setting a time for prayer, we need a way of quieting ourselves and coming to an awareness of God's presence. We must "tune out" any interference and "tune in" God. There are many ways to do this. You may wish to use the following method:

- Sit quietly in a firm chair. Keep your back straight. Close your eyes and become aware of any tension. Relax the muscles in your face, neck, shoulders, arms, torso, legs, and feet. Reflect on the words of Jesus, "Peace I leave with you; my peace I give to you" (John 14:27).
- Pay attention to your breathing. If it is shallow, deepen it. If it is rapid, slow it down. Breathe deeply and try to feel the air entering your lungs. Think for a moment about the first breath you took as a baby and about the last breath you will take on this earth. Reflect on this verse of Scripture: "The breath of the Almighty keeps me alive" (Job 33:4).
- Be attentive to the sounds of life around you, perhaps a bird singing, a breeze stirring the trees, voices in the distance, a car passing. Think of how all activity and life have their origin in God. Meditate on these words: "Listen to the voice of the LORD your God" (Jeremiah 26:13).
- Be sensitive to the experience of touch. Feel the softness of your clothing, the press of the chair against your body and of the floor against your feet, even the gentle embrace of the air surrounding you. Think about these words of Paul, "In him we live and move and have our being" (Acts 17:28).
- Try to feel your heart beating. Think of how it pumps life-giving oxygen to every cell in your body. Think, too, of how the human heart is a symbol of love, just as necessary for life as a healthy heart. Ponder these words of Scripture: God has "set his heart on you" (Deuteronomy 7:7); "You shall love the Lord your God with all your heart" (Mark 12:30).

## Pathways to Prayer:
## Speaking to God in Private Prayer (C 2697–2724)

After we have become attentive to God's voice, how should we reply? The most natural way is to talk to God in our own words. There are four basic types of prayer: praise, thanks, sorrow, and petition. Elegant phrases are not required. We need only be open and honest, saying what is really in our hearts. Whether we are happy or sad, angry or at peace, we can share our feelings with God. We may vocalize our prayer, or we may speak in the silence of our hearts.

Another common way to respond to God is to use formulas of prayer. Many such formulas may be found in the Bible, as noted above. Others, like the Hail Mary and Prayer of Praise, have been passed down for centuries and are memorized by most Catholics. There are books of prayers for every occasion and circumstance in life, and many Catholics have a favorite prayer book.

Certain kinds of prayer patterns have been popular with Catholics for generations. The rosary is said using beads to count recital of the Lord's Prayer, ten Hail Marys, and the Prayer of Praise, while we reflect on mysteries from the lives of Jesus and Mary. The Way of the Cross is a devotion at which we meditate on the sufferings of Jesus during his Passion and death, and the stations may be seen on the walls of many Catholic churches.

Catholics also pray without words, using the many forms of mental prayer developed by saints and spiritual guides. One of the best known is that taught by Saint Ignatius of Loyola. After directing our attention to God, we reflect, for example, on some scene from the gospels. We place ourselves in the scene, imagining the sights and sounds. We talk with Jesus. We make some practical resolution as a result of our reflection. Another method is reflective reading, wherein we read from the Bible or a spiritual book, pausing to think and pray each time some passage inspires us. Another is the Jesus Prayer, where we gently and slowly pray the name of Jesus, focusing on his presence and love. The techniques given under "Pathways to Prayer: Attentiveness to God" may be used to prepare ourselves for other forms of meditation, or they may be employed for a long time as our prayer. Mental prayer can also be simple and contemplative: we place ourselves before God in silence, content just to be with the Lord.

"Imaging prayer" is a kind of contemplative prayer. In this prayer we focus on images rather than words. We praise God by picturing ourselves kneeling before the throne of God in heaven. We thank God by visualizing the blessings we have received as gifts flowing to us from God. We express sorrow for sin by mentally standing at the cross of Jesus. We make petitions by forming images of our needs and placing them before God. We pray for others by picturing Jesus standing next to them, placing his hands on them and blessing them. "Imaging prayer" is a beautiful way to end our day. After retiring, we visualize Jesus standing watch over people who need his help and over ourselves as we sleep.

Some people keep prayer journals, a daily record of prayer, and may make their prayer to God in writing. If we can send thoughts and feelings to people through letters, we can surely direct them to God in prayer journals.

### Pathways to Prayer: Speaking to God
### Through Prayer in Common (C 1074–78, 2685–90, 2790–93)

Most methods of prayer may be used not only by individuals but also by groups of people, and so become common prayer. There is a special value to prayer with others, as we learn from Jesus, "Where two or three are gathered together in my name, there am I in the midst of them" (Matthew 18:20).

The official communal prayer of the Church, and our most important prayer, is the liturgy. This includes the Mass and the sacraments, Benediction, and the Liturgy of the Hours. Sunday Mass should be the heart of all our prayer, and many Catholics attend daily Mass as a way to unite their lives to Christ. All celebrations of the sacraments are prayer and allow us to pray for ourselves and others at key moments in life. Benediction is worship, through song and prayer, of Christ present in the Blessed Sacrament. The Liturgy of the Hours is the daily prayer of the Church, said by priests, religious, and many laypeople.

In many Catholic parishes there are prayer groups that meet regularly. Some recite the rosary. Others study the Bible, then pray and sing together. There are charismatic prayer groups that pay special attention to the gifts of the Holy Spirit, including praying in tongues (1 Corinthians 12–14).

There are many retreat and renewal movements in the Catholic Church today. Some religious orders sponsor retreats for laypeople.

There are Marriage Encounter Weekends for married couples, Teens Encounter Christ retreats for young people, Beginning Again Weekends for the widowed and divorced. Such movements encourage participants to meet for prayer and reflection on a regular basis.

Singing is an important form of common prayer. It is often a part of liturgical prayer, especially the Mass. Through singing, we direct melody and words to God as praise, thanks, contrition, or petition. (We may use music in private prayer also. Some listen to recorded religious music as a way to lift mind and heart to God, and some sing favorite hymns to express their feelings to God.)

In today's world there is a special need for family prayer. "The family that prays together stays together." Modern families must realize that prayer is not a luxury but a necessity. We find time for things that are important, and we simply must find time for prayer. Even the busiest families can take a few minutes after the evening meal to read and discuss the Bible or to pray one decade of the rosary or to pray about the events of the day.

### Attitudes Toward Prayer (C 2725–51)

Our first attitude should be an openness to all that God tells us about prayer in the Scriptures. Focusing on one passage to the exclusion of others can give a distorted view of prayer. For example, Mark 11:24, "All that you ask for in prayer, believe that you will receive it and it shall be yours," must be interpreted in the light of Jesus' other statements, especially those counseling submission to God's will. There is an old saying that God always answers prayers, but sometimes the answer is "yes," sometimes "no," and sometimes "wait."

A second attitude is that we must pray in accord with the ordinary laws of life and common sense. If I pray, "Lord, help our basketball team to win this game," I am asking God to be on our team. God might respond, "Only five players are allowed on a team!" A better prayer might be, "Lord, help us to do our best." Prayers to win a game or a lottery ask God to give us an unfair advantage.

A third attitude has to do with the degree of faith with which we pray. On the one hand it is a mistake to blame ourselves for lack of faith every time a petition seems to go unanswered. On the other hand it is probably a mistake to assume that our faith is all it should be. Perhaps our prayers might be more effective if our faith were stronger. Without worrying, we should ask God for the grace of faith, then pray, entrusting the answer to God's providence.

A fourth attitude is also faith-related. Often we lack confidence, not because God fails to answer our prayers, but because we do not recognize God's answers. We are given what we ask, then wonder if it wasn't just a coincidence. (Someone has observed: "Coincidences happen more often when I pray!") Or we forget how often prayers are answered. If we kept a journal of our requests and the answers received, our confidence in God might be enhanced.

A fifth attitude is the awareness that God cannot answer some prayers because we build up walls between ourselves and God. We cannot receive forgiveness from God unless we are willing to forgive those who offend us (Matthew 18:21-35). We sever communications with God by sin, whereas we open ourselves to God's blessings by holiness of life (1 John 3:21-22).

A sixth attitude: God may not answer our prayer as we'd like because we should take responsibility for answering that prayer. When we pray, "Lord, help the poor," God may suggest that we help the poor by sharing. When we ask God for good health, God may respond by urging us to give up unhealthy habits and get more exercise!

Seventh, we should realize that not all people have the same gifts. Some have a special ability to know what to ask for. Some have a gift of praying for the sick. Some report they can "hear" God speaking to them. There are many spiritual gifts, and no one possesses them all. Many individuals with many kinds of spiritual gifts make up the Body of Christ (1 Corinthians 12:12-31).

An eighth attitude has been expressed in the phrase, "The purpose of prayer is not to bring God around to our way of thinking but to bring us around to God's way of thinking." God's way of thinking may not be ours. We may pray that God will take away an illness or disability and receive instead the patience and strength to endure, as Paul did (2 Corinthians 12:7-9). Often, as believers become more experienced in the ways of prayer, they find themselves asking for fewer things and are content simply to place their lives in God's hands.

A ninth attitude is the awareness that we pray to open ourselves to the blessings God wants us to have. This is true of prayers of praise, thanksgiving, petition, and sorrow for sin. Our praise and thanks do not benefit God, but put us in a proper relationship to our Creator. We make petitions not to persuade God, but to turn toward God as the source of all good. We express sorrow not to convince God to forgive us, but to open our hearts to the pardon God offers through Jesus.

A tenth attitude is that we can pray with more assurance for spiritual blessings than for material benefits. Jesus says, "If you then, who are wicked, know how to give good gifts to your children, how much more will the Father in heaven give the holy Spirit to those who ask him?" (Luke 11:13). We may pray for prosperity, but such a prayer might merit a positive answer less than a prayer for humility! Further, there are complications in praying for material blessings: the rain we want to make our garden grow might wash out our neighbor's picnic.

An eleventh attitude realizes that God respects the free will of those for whom we pray. If they have hardened their hearts, they can refuse the grace God offers them in answer to our prayers. Still, persevering prayer can have a great effect on sinners, as when Saint Augustine was converted after years of prayer by his mother, Saint Monica. Like a farmer who digs one irrigation channel after another, sending water to moisten arid fields, a believer praying for a wayward friend establishes channels through which God's grace can soften the hardest heart.

The twelfth is an attitude which keeps us open to exciting possibilities for prayer. Today much research is being done into the activity of the right side of the human brain and into the communication of feelings and ideas through the right side of the brain. Identical twins often seem to be able to communicate without words and to feel emotions experienced by each other. Perhaps we have such abilities that can be developed through prayer. Just as we have learned to harness electricity to power our machines, so perhaps we can learn to use prayer to strengthen our relationships with one another and to experience the power of God.

### Better Than *Voyager 2* (C 2752–58)

We can make comparisons between modern communications and prayer, but while *Voyager 2* will remain in empty space for the next one hundred thousand years and may never be seen by another creature, our contact with God through prayer is instantaneous and certain!

Prayer can also be difficult. At times God seems close, then very far away. After a retreat we may feel that we have reached the heights of perfect prayer, but God may then withdraw to lead us higher still. Even the saints had periods of fervor and dryness, and their example encourages us to persevere in prayer.

When we attune ourselves to the many ways in which God speaks to us, when we become aware of the many opportunities we have to speak with God, we leave the narrow confines of planet Earth and open ourselves to the infinite love and power of God. Prayer is not just a "close encounter." Prayer "joins heaven to earth, and earth to heaven."

## The Light Shines in the Darkness (C 1061–65)

Our story of the Catholic Church began with the vastness and beauty of the universe, created by God from the darkness of nothing. It concludes with prayer that joins earth to heaven itself! God wants us to be led through the great goodness of this world into the full light of God's presence (John 1:5). There is sin and darkness on this earth, surely, but Christ our Light has turned the darkness into day. In every age members of the Catholic Church, with all their faults and failings, have tried to be faithful to the Lord. Now we have the privilege of being part of that Church, the Body of Christ, as the Light continues to shine.

### *Questions for Discussion or Reflection*

Have you ever thought of prayer as an adventure even more exciting than trying to communicate with beings from another planet? Can you think of times when you received answers to prayer in a remarkable way? Mention has been made of prayer of praise, thanksgiving, sorrow, and petition. Which of these kinds of prayer do you say most often? Least often? Of the various "attitudes" toward prayer given in this chapter, which seems most important to you? Are there any attitudes given that you disagree with? Which of the pathways to private prayer have you used? Are there any that you would like to try more often?

### *Activities*

Use the prayer exercises suggested under "Pathways to Prayer: Attentiveness to God" (see page 199).

# BIBLIOGRAPHY

Abbott, Walter, editor. *The Documents of Vatican II*. New York: Herder and Herder, 1966.

Adler, Mortimer. *How to Think About God*. New York: Bantam Books, 1991.

*Catechism of the Catholic Church*. United States Catholic Conference, 1994.

*Handbook for Today's Catholic*. Liguori, MO: Liguori Publications. 1994.

John Paul II. *The Splendor of Truth*. Boston: St. Paul Books, 1993.

Lewis, C.S. *Mere Christianity*. New York: Macmillan, 1986.

Lukefahr, Oscar. *A Catholic Guide to the Bible*. Liguori, MO: Liguori Publications, 1992.

____. *Morning Star...Christ's Mother and Ours*. Liguori, MO: Liguori Publications, 1995.

____. *The Privilege of Being Catholic*. Liguori, MO: Liguori Publications, 1993.

*New American Bible*. Brookville, NY: Catholic Book Publisher, 1970, 1989, 1991.

*New American Bible — Revised New Testament*. Twelve cassette tape set. Hosanna, 2421 Aztec Road NE, Albuquerque, NM 87107. Phone 1-800-545-6552.

*New Catholic Encyclopedia*. New York: McGraw-Hill Book Company, 1967.

# INDEX